ZEN
FOR
AMERICANS

TRANSLATED BY
D. T. SUZUKI

ZEN
FOR
AMERICANS
Including THE SUTRA OF
FORTY-TWO CHAPTERS

SOYEN
SHAKU

MetroBooks

This is an unabridged reprint of the 1913 edition entitled *Sermons of a Buddhist*.

This edition published by **Metro**Books,
an imprint of Friedman/Fairfax Publishers.

2002 **Metro**Books

ISBN 1-5866-3563-8

Printed and bound in the United States of America

02 03 04 05 MC 18 17 16 15 14 13

FG

For bulk purchases and special sales, please contact:
Friedman/Fairfax Publishers
Attention: Sales Department
230 Fifth Avenue, Suite 700-701
New York, NY 10001
212/685-6610 Fax 212/685-3916

Visit our website:
www.metrobooks.com

TRANSLATOR'S PREFACE

THIS little work is a collection of some of the lectures delivered by the Right Reverend Soyen Shaku, Lord Abbot of Engaku-ji and Kencho-ji, Kamakura, Japan, during his sojourn in this country, 1905–1906. He came here early in the summer of 1905 and stayed with friends on the Pacific coast until March in the following year. Lectures on Buddhism were frequently delivered at the request of his hostess, Mrs. Alexander Russell of San Francisco, for the benefit of her friends. He lectured on the *Sutra of Forty-two Chapters*, and naturally chose the texts for his sermons from this most popular among the canonical books. As His Reverence did not speak English, the burden of interpreting his speeches fell upon my shoulders.

During his stay on the coast, His Reverence was occasionally invited by his countrymen, scattered throughout the State, to such places as the Buddhist Mission and the Japanese Consulate in San Francisco, to Los Angeles, Sacramento, Fresno, San Jose, and Oakland. Wherever he went, his addresses were most enthusiastically received and greatly appreciated by

iii

the Japanese residents, and by Americans when his speeches were repeated in English.

In March, 1906, the Right Reverend Soyen Shaku crossed the continent to the Atlantic coast, visiting Washington, New York, Philadelphia, and Boston. Whenever he was asked by his countrymen or by his American friends to speak on his faith, he always acceded to their wish. These addresses were added to the sermons already under my charge, and when His Reverence was leaving for his European tour towards the end of April, he left all the manuscripts with me with a view of publishing them in book form.

In going over these documents critically, I found that I could not make use of all the material as it stood; for the talks during his stay on the Pacific coast were mostly of a very informal nature, and a copy of them prepared from shorthand notes needed a great deal of revision; besides, some of the talks were suited only to special audiences and adapted to their peculiar needs. So with his permission I condensed several articles into one, while in other cases I selected a subject only incidentally or cursorily referred to in several different addresses, and made a special essay of the scattered passages. Sometimes I found his expressions too Buddhistic, that is, too technical, and intelligible only to those who have made Buddhism a special study. In such cases, I put the thoughts in a more conventional and comprehensible form for the benefit of the American public. Again, when I thought that His Reverence took too much knowledge of his subject for granted on the part of his audience, I endeavored to express his thoughts more plainly and explicitly.

In spite of these alterations and the liberties I have taken with the manuscripts of the Reverend Shaku, these lectures remain a faithful representation of the views as well as the style of preaching of my venerable teacher and friend.

*   *   *

As to the text of the *Sutra of Forty-two Chapters*, I have decided after much consideration to incorporate it here. In the first place, it is not a long sutra, and like the *Dharmapada* it contains many characteristic Buddhist thoughts. Secondly, most of the Reverend Shaku's lectures have a close relation to the sutra; and when they are read after the perusal of the text, his standpoint as a modern Japanese representative of Buddhism will be better understood. Thirdly, being the first Buddhist literature introduced by the first official Hindu missionaries into the Middle Kingdom (A. D. 67), the sutra has a very interesting historical background.

*   *   *

I have to add that this collection also contains two articles and one letter by the Reverend Shaku, all of which previously appeared in THE OPEN COURT. The letter was addressed to the

late Dr. John H. Barrows as a sort of protest
against his lecture delivered at the Chicago University, 1896, in which Dr. Barrows unfortunately
fell in line with the popular misconception of the
spirit of Buddhism. The two articles referred
to deal with the problem of war as seen from the
general Buddhist point of view; and I may remark
that the first of the two attracted at the time the
attention of such an eminent thinker of our day
as Count Leo Tolstoy and was alluded to in his
famous anti-war declaration.

DAISETZ TEITARO SUZUKI.

La Salle, Ill., 1906.

CONTENTS

THE SUTRA OF FORTY-TWO CHAPTERS

THE SUTRA OF FORTY-TWO CHAPTERS[1]

HAVING attained Buddhahood, the World-honored One thought thus: "To be free from the passions and to be calm, this is the most excellent Way."

---

[1]This is the first Buddhist literature ever translated into the Chinese language. It was brought into China by the first missionaries from Central India, A. D. 67, who were specially invited by the Emperor Ming of the Han Dynasty. Though some authorities think that the sutra existed in Sanskrit in the present Chinese form, the most probable fact is, as maintained by another authority, that the translators extracted all these passages from the different Buddhist canonical books which they brought along for their missionary purposes, and compiled them after the fashion of the Confucian *Analects*, beginning each chapter with the stereotyped "The Buddha said," which corresponds to the Confucian "The Master said." This was the most natural thing for the first Buddhist workers from India to do in the land of Confucianism.

The sutra, besides being a collection of moral and religious sayings of the Buddha, is interesting to us at least in the following two points: (1) It throws some light on the development which Buddhism made in India from the Parinirvâna of Buddha down to the times of these two translators; and (2) it allows us to see what the first Buddhist propagandists thought best to introduce, as the most essen-

He was absorbed in Great Meditation,[1] sub-
dued all evil ones, and in Deer Park[2] caused to
revolve the Wheel of Dharma, which was the
Fourfold Truth,[3] and converted the five Bhikshus,[4] Kaudinya, etc., inducing them to attain
Enlightenment.[5]

Again, there were other Bhikshus who implored the Buddha to remove their doubts
which they had concerning his doctrine. The
World-honored One illumined all their minds
through his authoritative teachings. The Bhik-

---

tial doctrines of their faith, among the people who had
hitherto been educated mostly by the Confucians but partly
by the Laotzeans.

The first translators did not think it wise to present their
doctrine systematically by writing a discourse or a lengthy
treatise, as they were wont to do in their native country,
nor did they think it advisable to reproduce an entire sutra
in the language of their newly adopted country. On the
other hand, they culled Buddha's short sayings and dialogues
from various sutras, imitating the general style of the Confucian sacred book *Lun Yu*. They must have thought that
Buddhism, which has so many voluminous canonical books
and deeply metaphysical treatises, would be best promul-
gated in China through an anthology, and not through an
exact reproduction of the original texts. The present sutra
is undoubtedly the result of these considerations, and on
this account it must be said to be well suited for popular
reading.

[1]Cf. "The Practice of Dhâna." (P. 146.)

[2]"The Story of Deer Park" is told elsewhere. (P. 182.)

[3]This is explained in the article entitled "The Wheel of
the Good Law." (P. 101.)

[4]Buddhist monks are called Bhikshus, literally "beggars."

[5]What the Buddhists understand by Enlightenment is
explained in the sermons. (See p. 132.)

shus, joining their hands and reverentially bowing, followed his august instructions.

(1) The Buddha said: "Those who leave their parents, go out of the home, understand the mind, reach the source, and comprehend the immaterial, are called Çramana.[1]

"Those who observe the two hundred and fifty precepts[2] of morality, who are pure and spotless in their behavior, and who exert themselves for the attainment of the four fruits of saintship,[3] are called Arhats.

"The Arhat is able to fly through space and assume different forms; his life is eternal, and there are times when he causes heaven and earth to quake.[4]

"Next is the Anâgâmin.[5] At the end of his life, the spirit of the Anâgâmin ascends to the nineteenth heaven and obtains Arhatship.

"Next is the Skridâgâmin.[6] The Skridâgâmin

---

[1]Or Çramanera, from the root çram, "to exert oneself,"; "to make effort."

[2]This is fully explained in the Vinaya texts in the Sacred Books of the East, Vols. XIII, XVII, XX.

[3]The Arhats, the Anâgamins, the Skridâgamins, the Srotâpannas. These are explained below.

[4]This and the following three passages seem to be a gloss, incorporated in the text later by a copyist. Arhat, according to the traditional Chinese interpretation, means "one who kills robbers," that is, the robbers of passion and prejudice.

[5]Anâgâmin means "one who never returns." The nineteenth heaven is called Akanishtha, the highest in the world of form (rûpaloka).

[6]Skridâgâmin means "one who comes back."

ascends to the heavens [after his death], comes
back to the earth once more, and then attains
Arhatship.

"Next is the Srotaâpanna.¹ The Srotaâpanna
dies seven times and is born seven times, when
he finally attains Arhatship.

"By the severance of the passions is meant
that like the limbs severed they are never again
made use of."

(2) The Buddha said: "The homeless Çramana cuts off the passions, frees himself of
attachments, understands the source of his own
mind, penetrates the deepest doctrine of Buddha,
and comprehends the Dharma which is immaterial.
He has no prejudice in his heart, he has nothing
to hanker after. He is not hampered by the
thought of the Way, nor is he entangled in karma.
No prejudice, no compulsion, no discipline, no
enlightenment, and no going up through the
grades, and yet in possession of all honors in
itself,—this is called the Way."

(3) The Buddha said: "Those who shaving
their heads and faces become Çramanas and who
receive instruction in the Way, should surrender
all worldly possessions and be contented with
whatever they obtain by begging.² One meal a
day and one lodging under a tree, and neither
should be repeated. For what makes one stupid
and irrational is attachments and the passions."

¹Srotaâpanna means "one who gets in the stream."
²Cf. Luke, xii, 33 *et seq.*

(4) The Buddha said: "There are ten things considered good by all beings, and ten things evil. What are they? Three of them depend upon the body, four upon the mouth, and three upon thought.

"Three evil deeds depending upon the body are: killing, stealing, and committing adultery. The four depending upon the mouth are: slandering, cursing, lying, and flattery. The three depending upon thought are: envy, anger, and infatuation. All these things are against the Holy Way, and therefore they are evil.

"When these evils are not done, there are ten good deeds."

(5) The Buddha said: "If a man who has committed many a misdemeanor does not repent and cleanse his heart of the evil, retribution will come upon his person as sure as the streams run into the ocean which becomes ever deeper and wider.

"If a man who has committed a misdemeanor come to the knowledge of it, reform himself, and practise goodness, the force of retribution will gradually exhaust itself as a disease gradually loses its baneful influence when the patient perspires."

(6) The Buddha said: "When an evil-doer, seeing you practise goodness, comes and maliciously insults you, you should patiently endure it and not feel angry with him, for the evil-doer is insulting himself by trying to insult you."

(7) The Buddha said: "Once a man came unto me and denounced me on account of my observing the Way and practising great loving-kindness. But I kept silent and did not answer him. The denunciation ceased. I then asked him, 'If you bring a present to your neighbor and he accepts it not, does the present come back to you?' The man replied, 'It will.' I said, 'You denounce me now, but as I accept it not, you must take the wrong deed back on your own person. It is like echo succeeding sound, it is like shadow following object; you never escape the effect of your own evil deeds. Be therefore mindful, and cease from doing evil.'"

(8) The Buddha said: "Evil-doers who denounce the wise resemble a person who spits against the sky; the spittle will never reach the sky, but comes down on himself. Evil-doers again resemble a man who stirs the dust against the wind; the dust is never raised without doing him injury. Thus, the wise will never be hurt, but the curse is sure to destroy the evil-doers themselves."

(9) The Buddha said: "If you endeavor to embrace the Way through much learning, the Way will not be understood. If you observe the Way with simplicity of heart, great indeed is this Way."

(10) The Buddha said: "Those who rejoice in seeing others observe the Way will obtain great blessing." A Çramana asked the Buddha,

"Would this blessing ever be destroyed?" The Buddha said, "It is like a lighted torch whose flame can be distributed to ever so many other torches which people may bring along; and therewith they will cook food and dispel darkness, while the original torch itself remains burning ever the same It is even so with the bliss of the Way."

(11) The Buddha said: "It is better to feed one good man than to feed one hundred bad men. It is better to feed one who observes the five precepts of Buddha than to feed one thousand good men. It is better to feed one Srotaâpanna than to feed ten thousands of those who observe the five precepts of Buddha. It is better to feed one Skridâgâmin than to feed one million of Srotaâpannas. It is better to feed one Anâgâmin than to feed ten millions of Skridâgâmins. It is better to feed one Arhat than to feed one hundred millions of Anâgâmins. It is better to feed one Pratyekabuddha than to feed one billion of Arhats. It is better to feed one of the Buddhas, either of the present, or of the past, or of the future, than to feed ten billions of Pratyekabuddhas. It is better to feed one who is above knowledge, onesidedness, discipline, and enlightenment than to feed one hundred billions of Buddhas of the past, present, or future."[1]

---

[1]This seems to be a very sweeping assertion on the part of the Buddha, but the principle remains ever true. The

(12) The Buddha said: "There are twenty difficult things to attain [or to accomplish] in this world: (1) It is difficult for the poor to practise charity; (2) It is difficult for the strong and rich to observe the Way;[1] (3) It is difficult to disregard life and go to certain death; (4) It is only a favored few that get acquainted with a Buddhist sutra; (5) It is by rare opportunity that a person is born in the age of Buddha; (6) It is difficult to conquer the passions, to suppress selfish desires; (7) It is difficult not to hanker after that which is agreeable; (8) It is difficult not to get into a passion when slighted; (9) It is difficult not to abuse one's authority; (10) It is difficult to be even-minded and simple-hearted in all one's dealings with others; (11) It is difficult to be thorough in learning and exhaustive in investigation; (12) It is difficult to subdue selfish pride; (13) It is difficult not to feel contempt toward the unlearned; (14) It is difficult to be one in knowledge and practice; (15) It is difficult not to express an opinion about others;[2] (16) It is by rare opportunity that one

---

fundamental fact of the religious life is purity of heart. If there is a dark corner in your heart, all that you do is hypocrisy. When the Emperor Wu of Liang saw Bodhidharma, he asked the saint, "I have built so many monasteries, I have converted so many souls, I have copied so many sacred sutras; now what does Your Holiness think my merit will be?" To this, Bodhidharma made a curt response, "No merit whatever."

[1]Cf. Matt. xix, 24.   [2]Cf. Matt. vii, 1, 2.

is introduced to a true spiritual teacher; (17) It is difficult to gain an insight into the nature of being and to practise the Way; (18) It is difficult to follow the steps of a savior; (19) It is difficult to be always the master of oneself; (20) It is difficult to understand thoroughly the Ways of Buddha."

(13) A monk asked the Buddha: "Under what conditions is it possible to come to the knowledge of the past and to understand the most supreme Way?" The Buddha said: "Those who are pure in heart and single in purpose are able to understand the most supreme Way. It is like polishing a mirror, which becomes bright when the dust is removed. Remove your passions, and have no hankering, and the past will be revealed unto you."

(14) A monk asked the Buddha: "What is good, and what is great?" The Buddha answered: "Good is to practise the Way and to follow the truth. Great is the heart that is in accord with the Way."

(15) A monk asked the Buddha: "What is most powerful, and what is most illuminating?" The Buddha said: "Meekness is most powerful, for it harbors no evil thoughts, and, moreover, it is restful and full of strength. As it is free from evils, it is sure to be honored by all.[1]

"The most illuminating is a mind which is

[1] Matt. v, 5.

thoroughly cleansed of dirt, and which, remaining pure, retains no blemishes. From the time when there was yet no heaven and earth till the present day, there is nothing in the ten quarters which is not seen, or known, or heard by such a mind, for it has gained all-knowledge, and for that reason it is called 'illuminating.'"

(16) The Buddha said: "Those who have passions are never able to perceive the Way; for it is like stirring up clear water with hands; people may come there wishing to find a reflection of their faces, which, however, they will never see. A mind troubled and vexed with the passions is impure, and on that account it never sees the Way. O monks, do away with passions. When the dirt of passion is removed the Way will manifest itself."

(17) The Buddha said: "Seeing the Way is like going into a dark room with a torch; the darkness instantly departs, while the light alone remains. When the Way is attained and the truth is seen, ignorance vanishes and enlightenment abides forever."

(18) The Buddha said: "My doctrine is to think the thought that is unthinkable, to practise the deed that is not-doing, to speak the speech that is inexpressible, and to be trained in the discipline that is beyond discipline. Those who understand this are near, those who are confused are far. The Way is beyond words and expressions, is bound by nothing earthly. Lose

sight of it to an inch, or miss it for a moment, and we are away from it forevermore."

(19) The Buddha said: "Look up to heaven and down on earth, and they will remind you of their impermanency. Look about the world, and it will remind you of its impermanency. But when you gain spiritual enlightenment, you shall then find wisdom. The knowledge thus attained leads you anon to the Way."

(20) The Buddha said: "You should think of the four elements[1] of which the body is composed. Each of them has its own name, and there is no such thing there known as ego. As there is really no ego, it is like unto a mirage."[2]

(21) The Buddha said: "Moved by their selfish desires, people seek after fame and glory. But when they have acquired it, they are already stricken in years. If you hanker after worldly fame and practise not the Way, your labors are wrongfully applied and your energy is wasted. It is like unto burning an incense stick. However much its pleasing odor be admired, the fire that consumes is steadily burning up the stick."

(22) The Buddha said: "People cleave to their worldly possessions and selfish passions so

---

[1]Earth, water, fire, and air.
[2]A Japanese poet sings:
> "When pulled together
> And bound, there stands
> A hut well thatched:
> But take it apart,
> And we have the wilderness eternal."

blindly as to sacrifice their own lives for them.
They are like a child who tries to eat a little
honey smeared on the edge of a knife. The
amount is by no means sufficient to appease his
appetite, but he runs the risk of wounding his
tongue."

(23) The Buddha said: "Men are tied up to
their families and possessions more helplessly
than in a prison. There is an occasion for the
prisoner to be released, but householders enter-
tain no desire to be relieved from the ties of
family. When a man's passion is aroused nothing prevents him from ruining himself. Even
into the maws of a tiger will he jump. Those
who are thus drowned in the filth of passion are
called the ignorant. Those who are able to
overcome it are saintly Arhats."

(24) The Buddha said: "There is nothing like
lust. Lust may be said to be the most powerful
passion. Fortunately, we have but one thing
which is more powerful. If the thirst for truth
were weaker than passion, how many of us in the
world would be able to follow the way of righteousness?"

(25) The Buddha said: "Men who are
addicted to the passions are like the torch-
carrier running against the wind; his hands are
sure to be burned."

(26) The Lord of Heaven offered a beautiful
fairy to the Buddha, desiring to tempt him to the
evil path. But the Buddha said, "Be gone.

What use have I for the leather bag filled with filth which you have brought to me?" Then, the god reverently bowed and asked the Buddha about the essence of the Way, in which having been instructed by the Buddha, it is said, he attained the Srotaâpanna-fruit.

(27) The Buddha said: "Those who are following the Way should behave like a piece of timber which is drifting along a stream. If the log is neither held by the banks, nor seized by men, nor obstructed by the gods, nor kept in the whirlpool, nor itself goes to decay, I assure you that this log will finally reach the ocean. If monks walking on the Way are neither tempted by the passions, nor led astray by some evil influences, but steadily pursue their course for Nirvâna, I assure you that these monks will finally attain enlightenment."

(28) The Buddha said: "Rely not upon your own will. Your own will is not trustworthy. Guard yourselves against sensualism, for it surely leads to the path of evil. Your own will becomes trustworthy only when you have attained Arhatship."

(29) The Buddha said: "O monks, you should not see women.[1] [If you should have to see them], refrain from talking to them. [If you should have to talk], you should reflect in a right spirit: 'I am now a homeless mendicant. In the world of sin, I must behave myself like unto

[1]Matt. v, 28.

the lotus flower whose purity is not defiled by the mud. Old ones I will treat as my mother; elderly ones as elder sisters; younger ones as younger sisters; and little ones as daughters.' And in all this you should harbor no evil thoughts, but think of salvation."

(30) The Buddha said: "Those who walk in the Way should avoid sensualism as those who carry hay would avoid coming near the fire."

(31) The Buddha said: "There was once a man who, being in despair over his inability to control his passions, wished to mutilate himself.[1] The Buddha said to him: 'Better destroy your own evil thoughts than do harm to your own person. The mind is lord. When the lord himself is calmed the servants will of themselves be yielding. If your mind is not cleansed of evil passions, what avails it to mutilate yourself?'" Thereupon, the Buddha recited the gâthâ,

"Passions grow from the will,
    The will grows from thought and imagination:
    When both are calmed,
    There is neither sensualism nor transmigration."

The Buddha said, this gâthâ was taught before by Kâshyapabuddha.

(32) The Buddha said: "From the passions arise worry, and from worry arises fear. Away with the passions, and no fear, no worry."

(33) The Buddha said: "Those who follow

---

[1]Matt. v, 29 and 30.

the Way are like unto warriors who fight single-
handed with a multitude of foes. They may all
go out of the fort in full armor; but among them
are some who are faint-hearted, and some who
go halfway and beat a retreat, and some who are
killed in the affray, and some who come home
victorious. O monks, if you desire to attain
enlightenment, you should steadily walk in your
Way, with a resolute heart, with courage, and
should be fearless in whatever environment you
may happen to be, and destroy every evil influence that you may come across; for thus you
shall reach the goal."

(34) One night a monk was reciting a sutra
bequeathed by Kâshyapabuddha. His tone was
so mournful, and his voice so fainting, as if he
were going out of existence. The Buddha asked
the monk, "What was your occupation before
you became a homeless monk?" Said the monk,
"I was very fond of playing the guitar." The
Buddha said, "How did you find it when the
strings were too loose?" Said the monk, "No
sound is possible." "How when the strings
were too tight?" "They crack." "How when
they were neither too tight nor too loose?"
"Every note sounds in its proper tone." The
Buddha then said to the monk, "Religious discipline is also like unto playing the guitar. When
the mind is properly adjusted and quietly applied,
the Way is attainable; but when you are too
fervently bent on it, your body grows tired; and

when your body is tired, your spirit becomes weary; when your spirit is weary, your discipline will relax; and with the relaxation of discipline there follows many an evil. Therefore, be calm and pure, and the Way will be gained."

(35) The Buddha said: "When a man makes utensils out of a metal which has been thoroughly cleansed of dross, the utensils will be excellent. You monks, who wish to follow the Way, make your own hearts clean from the dirt of evil passion, and your conduct will be unimpeachable."

(36) The Buddha said: "Even if one escapes from the evil creations, it is one's rare fortune to be born as a human being. Even if one be born as human, it is one's rare fortune to be born as a man and not a woman.[1] Even if one be born a man, it is one's rare fortune to be perfect in all the six senses. Even if he be perfect in all the six senses, it is his rare fortune to be born in the middle kingdom. Even if he be born in the middle kingdom, it is his rare fortune to be born in the time of a Buddha. Even if he be born in the time of a Buddha, it is his rare fortune to see the enlightened. Even if he be able to see the enlightened, it is his rare fortune to have his heart awakened in faith. Even if he have faith, it is his rare fortune to awaken the heart of intelligence. Even if he awakens the heart of intelligence, it is his rare fortune to

---

[1] Cf. I Cor. xi, 3, 7, 8, 9.

realize a spiritual state which is above discipline and attainment."

(37) The Buddha said: "O children of Buddha! You are away from me ever so many thousand miles, but if you remember and think of my precepts, you shall surely gain the fruit of enlightenment. You may, standing by my side, see me alway, but if you observe not my precepts, you shall never gain enlightenment."

(38) The Buddha asked a monk, "How do you measure the length of a man's life?" The monk answered, "By days." The Buddha said, "You do not understand the Way."

The Buddha asked another monk, "How do you measure the length of a man's life?" The monk answered, "By the time that passes during a meal." The Buddha said, "You do not understand the way."

The Buddha asked a third monk, "How do you measure the length of a man's life?" The monk answered, "By the breath." The Buddha said, "Very well, you know the Way."

(39) The Buddha said, "Those who study the doctrine of the Buddhas will do well to believe and observe all that is taught by them. It is like unto honey; it is sweet within, it is sweet without, it is sweet throughout; so is the Buddhas' teaching."

(40) The Buddha said: "O monks, you must not walk on the Way as the ox that is attached to the wheel. His body moves, but his heart is

not willing. But when your hearts are in accord
with the Way, there is no need of troubling
yourselves about your outward demeanor."

(41) The Buddha said: "Those who practise
the Way might well follow the example of an ox
that marches through the deep mire carrying a
heavy load. He is tired, but his steady gaze,
looking forward, will never relax until he come
out of the mire, and it is only then that he takes
a respite. O monks, remember that passions
and sins are more than the filthy mire, and that
you can escape misery only by earnestly and
steadily thinking of the Way."

(42) The Buddha said: "I consider the dig-
nities of kings and lords as a particle of dust
that floats in the sunbeam. I consider the
treasure of precious metals and stones as bricks
and pebbles. I consider the gaudy dress of
silks and brocades as a worn-out rag. I consider
this universe as small as the holila (?) fruit. I
consider the lake of Anavatapta as a drop of
oil with which one smears the feet. I consider
the various methods of salvation taught by the
Buddhas as a treasure created by the imagination.
I consider the transcendental doctrine of Buddhism as precious metal or priceless fabric seen
in a dream. I consider the teaching of Buddhas
as a flower before my eyes. I consider the practice of Dhyâna as a pillar supporting the Mount
Sumeru. I consider Nirvâna as awakening from
a day dream or nightmare. I consider the strug-

gle between heterodox and orthodox as the antics of the six [mythical] dragons. I consider the doctrine of sameness as the absolute ground of reality. I consider all the religious works done for universal salvation as like the plants in the four seasons."

THE TEACHINGS
OF SOYEN SHAKU

THE GOD-CONCEPTION OF BUDDHISM[1]

A MONG the many critical opinions which
are passed upon Buddhism by Christian
or Western scholars, there are two which stand
out most conspicuously and most persistently.
One of them declares that Buddhism is a religion
which denies the existence of the soul, and the
other that it is atheistic or at best pantheistic,
which latter term implies what is practically
tantamount to the rejection of a God, that is,
a personal God as believed in by the Christians.
The object of this discourse is to see to what
extent the second criticism is, if at all, justifiable.
In other words, I propose here to elucidate the
Buddhist conception of God.

At the outset, let me state that Buddhism is
not atheistic as the term is ordinarily understood. It has certainly a God, the highest
reality and truth, through which and in which
this universe exists. However, the followers of
Buddhism usually avoid the term God, for it
savors so much of Christianity, whose spirit is

---

[1]It may be interesting for our readers to read in connection with this article Dr. Paul Carus's Buddhist story entitled
Amitâbha.

not always exactly in accord with the Buddhist interpretation of religious experience. Again, Buddhism is not pantheistic in the sense that it identifies the universe with God. On the other hand, the Buddhist God is absolute and transcendent; this world, being merely its manifestation, is necessarily fragmental and imperfect. To define more exactly the Buddhist notion of the highest being, it may be convenient to borrow the term very happily coined by a modern German scholar, "panentheism," according to which God is πᾶν καὶ ἕν (all and one) and more than the totality of existence.

One of the most fundamental beliefs of Buddhism is that all the multitudinous and multifarious phenomena in the universe start from, and have their being in, one reality which itself has "no fixed abode," being above spatial and temporal limitations. However different and separate and irreducible things may appear to the senses, the most profound law of the human mind declares that they are all one in their hidden nature. In this world of relativity, or *nânâtva* as Buddhists call it, subject and object, thought and nature, are separate and distinct, and as far as our sense-experience goes, there is an impassable chasm between the two which no amount of philosophizing can bridge. But the very constitution of the mind demands a unifying principle which is an indispensable hypothesis for our conception of phenomenality; and this hypothesis is called "the gate of sameness," *samatâ*, in contradistinction to "the gate of difference," *nânâtva*; and Buddhism declares that no philosophy or religion is satisfactory which does not recognize these two gates. In some measure the "gate of sameness" may be considered to correspond to "God" and the "gate of difference" to the world of individual existence.

Now, the question is, "How does Buddhism conceive the relation between these two entrances to the abode of Supreme Knowledge (*sambodhi*)?" And the answer to this decides the Buddhist attitude towards pantheism, theism, atheism, and what not.

To state it more comprehensively, Buddhism recognizes the coexistence and identity of the two principles, sameness and difference. Things are many and yet one; they are one and yet many. I am not thou, and thou art not I; and yet we are all one in essence. When one slays another, there is an actor, an act, and a sufferer, all distinct and separate; and yet

> "If the red slayer think he slays,
>   Or if the slain think he is slain,
> They know not well the subtle ways
>   I keep, and pass, and turn again."

Buddhism, therefore, says that while we have to acknowledge the world of particulars in which individuality predominates, we must not forget that looking through the gate of sameness all

distinctions and contradictions vanish in a higher
principle of unity.   A Japanese poet thus sings:

> "Rain and hail and ice and snow,
> Neither like the other. So!
> When they melt, however, lo,
> See one stream of water flow!"

Intellectually, the coexistence of the two
mutually excluding thoughts is impossible, for
the proposition, "Mine are not thine," cannot
be made at the same time the proposition,
"Mine are thine."   But here Buddhism is speaking of our inmost religious experience, which
deals directly with facts and not with their more
or less distorted intellectual reflections.   It is,
therefore, really idle to say that Buddhism is
pantheistic or atheistic or nihilistic.   Buddhism
is not a philosophical system, though it is the
most rational and intellectual religion in the
world.   What it proposes is to make clear facts
of the deepest spiritual life and to formulate a
doctrine which leads its followers to the path of
inward experience.

Thus, according to the proclamation of an
enlightened mind, God or the principle of sameness is not transcendent, but immanent in the
universe, and we sentient beings are manifesting
the divine glory just as much as the lilies of the
field.   A God who, keeping aloof from his creations, sends down his words of command through
specially favored personages, is rejected by
Buddhists as against the constitution of human

reason. God must be in us, who are made in his likeness. We cannot presume the duality of God and the world. Religion is not to go to God by forsaking the world, but to find him in it. Our faith is to believe in our essential oneness with him, and not in our sensual separateness. "God in us and we in him," must be made the most fundamental faith of all religion.

We must not, however, suppose that God is no more than the sum-total of individual existences. God exists even when all creations have been destroyed and reduced to a state of chaotic barrenness. God exists eternally, and he will create another universe out of the ruins of this one. To our limited intelligence there may be a beginning and an end of the worlds, but as God surveys them, being and becoming are one selfsame process. To him nothing changes, or, to state it rather paradoxically, he sees no change whatever in all the changes we have around us; all things are absolutely quiet in their eternal cycle of birth and death, growth and decay, combination and disintegration. This universe cannot exist outside of God, but God is more than the totality of individual existences; God is here as well as there, God is not only this but also that. As far as he is manifested in nature and mind, they glorify him, and we can have a glimpse of his image and feel, however imperfectly, his inner life. But it will be a grievous error, let us repeat, to think that he has exhausted his being in the manifestation of this universe, that he is absolutely identical with his creations, and that with the annihilation of the world he vanishes into eternal emptiness.

There is a favorite saying in Buddhism which declares that "sameness without difference is sameness wrongly conceived, while difference without sameness is difference wrongly conceived"; to express this in Christian terms, "God not in the world is a false God, and the world not in God is unreality." All things return to one, and one operates in all things; many in one and one in many; this is the Buddhist conception of God and the world. Billows and waves and ripples, all surging, swelling, and ebbing, and yet are they not so many different motions of the eternally selfsame body of water? The moon is serenely shining up in the sky, and she is alone in all the heavens and on the entire earth; but when she mirrors herself in the brilliant whiteness of the evening dews which appear like glittering pearls broadcast upon the earth from the hand of a fairy,—how wondrously numerous her images! And is not every one of them complete in its own fashion? This is the way in which an enlightened mind contemplates God and the world.

God is immanent in the world and not outside of it; therefore, when we comprehend the secret of the "little flower in the crannied wall," we know the reason of this universe. Reason is the inner life of all beings, it is the subjectivity of existence, it is the quickening spirit of all creation, it is a realization in our finite minds of infinite divinity. When we know ourselves, we know heaven and earth, we know God, we know everything and anything. We know his presence even in the most insignificant flower in the field which is trampled under foot by men and beasts carelessly and pitilessly, to say nothing about the starry heavens with their grandeur which is replete with suggestions, or about the huge mass of inert matter on which mountains rise, oceans roar, and sentient beings walk. When we come to realize this mysterious presence of the highest reason in all things, we are struck with the fact and there arise mingled feelings of awe, admiration, and helplessness, which latter is strangely tinged with a sense of self-exaltation. We are awe-stricken because it is beyond our human intelligence to grasp thoroughly the scheme of God. We admire it because of the wonderful beauty and harmony which are traceable in every step of his, though our imperfect minds are sometimes set against almost insurmountable difficulties in the reconciliation of contraries and opposites. We feel helpless because our fragmentary consciousness is unable to review the entire range of divine operation and thus to know the why of all these things, though the recognition of divinity in us lifts us above the wearisome condemnation piled upon humanity by some moralists and religionists.

*   *   *

Having thus expounded the Buddhist conception of God and his relation to us, I wish to proceed to explain some terms which are generally used by Buddhists to designate the highest being in its various modes and phases.

As I mentioned before, Buddhists do not make use of the term God, which characteristically belongs to Christian terminology. An equivalent most commonly used is Dharmakâya, which word has been explained in one of the sermons herein collected, and it will not be necessary to enter again upon the discussion of its signification. Let us only see what other equivalents have been adopted.

When the Dharmakâya is most concretely conceived it becomes the Buddha, or Tathâgata, or Vairochana, or Amitâbha. Buddha means "the enlightened," and this may be understood to correspond to "God is wisdom." Vairochana is "coming from the sun," and Amitâbha, "infinite light," which reminds us of the Christian notion, "God is light." As to the correct meaning of Tathâgata, Buddhists do not give any definite and satisfactory explanation, and it is usually considered to be the combination of *tathâ* ="thus" and *gata* ="gone," but it is difficult to find out how "Thus Gone" came to be an appellation of the supreme being. There are some scholars, however, who understand *gata* in the sense of "being in" or "situated in." If this be correct, Tathâgata meaning "being thus," or "being such," can be interpreted in the same sense as Tathâtâ or Bhûtatathâtâ or Tattva as explained below. But in this case Tathâgata will lose its personification and become a metaphysical term like the others, though it has been so persistently used by Buddhists in connection with the historical Buddha that it always awakens in their minds something more concrete and personal than a mere ontological abstraction.

Buddhism is the most speculative of all the existing religions in the world and abounds with many highly abstract terms which may sound empty to ordinary minds. Among them we have such words as Tathâtâ (or Tathâtva), Tattva, Bhûtatathâtâ, Bhûtakoti, Çûnyatâ, Alakshitam, Nirvâna, etc. These are all philosophical terms for Dharmakâya. To explain: Tathâtâ or tathâtva or tattva is "suchness," or "being such," and Buddhist scholars assert that, strictly speaking, these terms alone rightly designate the nature of the highest reality. When we speak of its absolute transcendentality, people are liable to take it for an empty nothing; while if we state that it is eternally true and real, they may consider it something concrete and particular. To avoid both extremes, or rather to synthesize them, the term "Suchness" has been coined; but in reality all human efforts are altogether insufficient to express the true nature of the ultimate. Says Açvaghosha, "The Immortal Essence is absolutely beyond intellectual demonstrability, but we as rational beings need some words to express ourselves, and for that purpose the term 'suchness' has been selected, disposing of all others." The words in which Goethe makes Faust utter his feeling concerning God may here be quoted also as corroborating Açvaghosha's conception of Suchness:

"Who dare express Him?
And who profess Him,
Saying: I believe in Him!
Who, feeling, seeing,
Deny this being,
Saying: I believe Him not!
The All-enfolding,
The All-upholding,
Folds and upholds He not
Thee, me, Himself?
    *   *   *
    *   *   *
Vast as it is, fill with that force thy heart,
And when thou in the feeling wholly blessed art,
Call it, then, what thou wilt,—
Call it Bliss! Heart! Love! God!
I have no name to give it!
Feeling is all in all:
The name is sound and smoke,
Obscuring Heaven's clear glow."

When even this Tathâtva is found inadequate for certain purposes, Buddhists add *Bhûta*= reality thereto and coin the word Bhûtatathâtâ, which means "that which really exists as such." Suchness, being an abstract term, may breed some misconception, when the term is used alone, on the part of the uninitiated. To avoid this, "reality" has been prefixed, which purposes to make it clear that the ultimate reason is not an abstraction, not a mere subjective creation, but a real objective (or rather transcendental) existence. Bhûtakoti serves the same end, as it means the "highest point of reality," or "the real end of things."

Alakshitam, Çûnyatâ, and Nirvânam express the negative phase of the Dharmakâya. When affirmation alone is not sufficient, we frequently resort to the negative way of defining things, showing thereby at least what they are not. The human mind cannot have a positively adequate conception of things which are beyond the realm of conditionality, for it is bound up within spatial and temporal relations; and in order to give expression to these non-conditional objects, we use the negative method and say that they are not such and such. In innumerable ways, this negation is as effective in defining things as affirmation.

When Buddhists assert that the Dharmakâya is çûnya = empty, or alakshana = devoid of particular marks, or nirvâna = emancipating, or nâçrava = faultless, they are following the inevitable course of mentation. All these and some other negative terms unfortunately have caused a great deal of misunderstanding on the part of unsympathetic critics who have either forgotten or ignored the peculiar proclivity of human reason to onesidedness and exclusiveness.

Lastly, Paramârtha and Satya are the terms used to designate the epistemological phase of the Dharmakâya. Paramârtha is the first or highest reason, and Satya is truth or that which truly is. And for the psychological aspect of the Dharmakâya, or as it is manifested in the human consciousness, we have Bodhi or Hridaya. Bodhi is the divine wisdom incarnated in our limited intelligence, or the divine love as reflected in our human sympathy and compassion. Hridaya is the inner life of existence which prompts and quickens us to do the will of the Dharmakâya, and which is awakened to its full dignity and glory when intelligence passes over the limits of relativity. The reason why we are able to have an insight into the nature of the ultimate being and to recognize the truth that sameness and difference are co-existent and really identical, is because our Bodhi or Hridaya is essentially one with the Dharmakâya. When the Bodhi comes to know itself, it also knows the inner being of Dharmakâya, however fragmentary the knowledge be, and we lie blissfully at rest in the bosom of eternal motherliness.

ASSERTIONS AND DENIALS

THERE are two avenues leading to the realization of the Buddhist life; one may be called positive and the other negative. They are complementary and mutually supporting. They are like the two sides of a shield, the two wings of a bird, or the two wheels of a cart. When one is asserted, the other necessarily follows as a logical consequence. What are they? The negative phase of Buddhism I may call the doctrine of the non-ego and the positive phase the doctrine of Dharmakâya (which latter may be considered to correspond to the Christian conception of God, though not exactly, as explained later).

Let me first expound the doctrine of the non-ego. Non-ego may not be a very appropriate term to express the Buddhist conception of Anâtman, but what I mean by this will become clearer, I hope, as I proceed. The Sanskrit term, Atman, which is generally translated by "ego," "self," "soul," or "individuality," is rather comprehensive and is used by different philosophical schools in different senses. Buddhists understand by Atman that something which, lurking behind all our mental experiences, directs them as it pleases, somehow after the fashion of an organist striking the notes as his whim or sentiment moves, or like a show-performer who makes his marionettes dance up and down according to his good pleasure. This strange something which is popularly supposed to be a concrete individual existence abiding somewhere within the body, and which is known by the masses as the ego or soul forming the central part of our existence, is denied by Buddhists as a superstitious belief, which has no foundation in reality. And this denial constitutes the negative side of Buddhism.

The absolute denial by Buddhism of the existence of the ego-soul may be somewhat startling to our Christian audience. They have been accustomed to such expressions as "the resurrection of the soul," "the immortality of the soul," "the redemption of the soul," "the reality of individuality," and so forth. Besides, we use the term "soul," or "ego," so constantly in our common parlance, taking the notion as the most positive fact, which does not allow of any doubt or refutation whatever. Our thoughts have thus become saturated, as it were, with the ego-conception; and when we see some one attempting to prove the phantasmagorial character of the ego or soul, we are unconsciously and unrestrainingly inclined to ridicule him. But let us stop for a moment and reflect seriously whether there is really such a thing as soul or self. Are we not deceiving ourselves when we condemn those who refuse to believe in the reality of self as agnostics, atheists, blasphemers, and charge them as immoral and faithless? Is not our own deception so fundamental and thorough-going as to put ourselves in a most puzzling position, difficult to extricate from when our cherished notion is brought out into the daylight and mercilessly examined by the tribunal of most advanced thoughts? Let us see how it is.

The first question I wish to ask is: "What do we understand by the soul or ego?" For instance, when we speak of the immortality of the soul, what mental image do we have about the soul? Do we not think that there is something, possibly within the body, as it cannot be abiding outside of us, which is so subtle and ethereal as to elude our gross senses, but which is a sort of concrete individual existence not belonging to any part of the body, and which departs from the latter when it breathes its last and either ascends to Heaven or goes into Hell, whereby this mythical entity receives its due and last judgment? As to the manner of its ascent or descent after the expiration of its earthly life, we are entirely ignorant, for no soul has ever come down among us to tell its unique experience, its flight through the air. It may be conceived that the soul performs this miraculous deed after the fashion of the Egyptian Ba, which is pictured commonly with two wings, earthly and material. Does such a ghostly being really reside within us? The very idea seems ridiculous.

We wanted to make the soul as immaterial as possible, but we have only succeeded in making it as material as any body which we have around us. For, however ethereal and astral the soul may be conceived, it cannot be anything but material, as long as it is concrete and individual. And for this reason I can declare that those self-advertising spiritualists are no more nor less than crass materialists,—the designation they wanted so much to hurl upon others.

Next, let us search in our own minds whether there abides such a thing as the self, to which we are so fatally attached. Is the will my self? Is intelligence my self? Are my ideas my self? Is consciousness my self? Are my numerous desires my self? My instincts? my judgment? my imagination? my experience? They are all my self in a sense, to be sure, but are they of such nature as to be thoroughly simple, constant, self-willing, and permanent, as we imagine the soul to be? Consciousness seems to be so, but are there not many occasions in our mental life when consciousness is altogether gone? And, again, are there not many cases of double or triple personality? In these cases, which consciousness shall I have to call my own real, permanent self or soul, which goes after my death to some unknown region? And, again, every one of us is acquainted with the fact that when I was a child I had a child-consciousness, that when I was a young man, I had a youth-consciousness, and that when I have grown to full manhood, I have a man-consciousness, and that when I am an old man, I shall have an old-man consciousness. My personality is thus constantly changing, in no case being the same. Which of these consciousnesses shall I call my real and true ego or soul and wish its immortality?

Of course, we have to admit that there is a unity of consciousness in our mental activities. But how fragile and inconstant is this so-called unity! This is so, not only in pathological cases, but in our normal condition. When I have an idea, I am the idea; when I have a desire, I am the desire; when I will, I am the will; for it is not warranted by experience to say that I have such and such thoughts or desires or impulses. But I am those thoughts or desires or impulses. I am constantly shifting from one thing to another, now a desire, now an idea, and so forth. However hard you may endeavor to catch this sort of "Wandering Jew," you will find it so slippery, so evasive, so inconstant, and finally you have to give it up as wasting labor.

A learned scholar was once very much troubled with the problem of the soul. He utterly lost peace of mind, and spent many years in agony and vexation, when at last he was informed of the news of the arrival of a saintly Buddhist

monk in his land. He hastened to the monas-
tery where the monk was settled in his temporary
sojourn, and most piteously implored him to be
instructed in spiritual discourse. The monk was,
however, apparently so absorbed in his contemplation that he did not even turn his head to
acknowledge a stranger. The scholar was not
disappointed, however, and it is said that he
stood at the same spot for a period of seven days
and nights. Finally, he drew a sword which he
carried in the belt as was the fashion of the time,
and cut off his own left arm, which he reverentially presented to the inscrutable mystic, saying:
"This is a token of my sincere desire to be
instructed in your religion. I have been search-
ing for my soul for so many years, and I am
indescribably vexed in my spirit. Please be
gracious enough to pacify my soul." The Buddhist monk then slowly turned toward the
supplicant and said, "Where is your soul? Bring
it to me, and I will have it pacified." The
scholar said, "The very trouble is that I cannot
find it." The monk exclaimed, "Pacified is
your soul!" and it happened that upon hearing
this a sort of spiritual flashlight went across the
mind of the scholar.

A favorite parable used by Buddhists to illustrate the unreality of soul or self (I take these
two meaning the same thing), is that of the house.
The house is composed of the roof, walls, posts,
floor, windows, and so forth. Now, take each

one. of these apart, and we have no such thing as a house, which appeared to have a permanent actuality awhile ago. The house did not have any independent existence outside the material whose combination only in a certain form makes it possible. From the beginning there was no house-soul or house-ego, which willed according to its own will to manifest itself in such and such way by combining the roofs, walls, et cetera. The house came into existence only after all these component parts were brought together. If the house-soul insisted that "I am a thing by itself, distinct from any of you, members of my being, and therefore I shall abide here forever even when you, component parts, are disorganized. I will go up to heaven and enjoy my reward there, for I have sheltered so many worthy people under my roof," this soul would be the most appropriate object of laughter and derision. But are we not standing in a similar situation when we speak of our eternal self dwelling within us and departing after death in its heavenward course?

*   *   *

So far the argument has been theoretical. Let me see the practical, ethical consequence of the ego-soul hypothesis. I find it producing most pernicious effects on our daily life, for the assertion of self-will, which is the root of all evil, is the logical, inevitable conclusion of the belief in the existence of a real ego-soul. But most people seem not to be aware of this fact. They

complain so much of the weakness of the flesh,
or the worldly inclinations of the "old man,"
but they do not endeavor to go to the bottom
of the matter and to find there the cause of all
spiritual vexations. When the cause is discovered the remedy is at hand. Let us ask, therefore: "What is the flesh? Who is the 'old man'?
Why does the flesh eternally interfere with the
aspirations and doings of the spirit? Why is
the flesh so meddlesome? Why has the old man
an evil eye on the new man?" When these
spirit-harassing questions are thoroughly inves-
tigated, we find that the arrogance of the flesh
is based on belief in the ultimate reality of the
ego-soul, that the impertinence of the "old man"
comes from the secret thought that the self is
real and abiding. "Crucify him," therefore,
says Buddhism, "as the first work in your
religious discipline; destroy this chimerical, illusory notion of self; get convinced of the truth
that there is no such creature dwelling in the
coziest corner of our minds; free yourselves from
the yoke of the ego-soul which exists not; and
you will see how vexatious and spirit-harrowing
it was to be confined within the self-made, self-
imposed prison. You will see again how free
and unhampered your life is in the ego-less
atmosphere where we all forget the limitations
of individualism and participate in the feeling
of universal brotherhood." The so-called "I"
is possible only when it is thought of in connection

with its fellow-selves. Indeed, this self and other selves are one in each other, I in you and you in me; and this sense of universal oneness breaks most effectually the barrier of egoism and glorifies the significance of individual existences. When we realize this exalted spirituality, we can truly say with the Gospel of John that "all mine are thine, and thine are mine; and I am glorified in them."

The conclusion thus here reached sheds light on another field of spiritual experience where many religionists are groping in the dark. They tell us that we must love our neighbors and even enemies. The injunction is noble, but we are not enlightened as to the reason why we must not assert ourselves to the destruction of enemies or to the disadvantage of neighbors. They simply insist that it is the command of a divine authority. This is very well with those who blindly accept it. But there are other religious people, often designated as heathens or pagans or atheists, who want to know the reason why. Seeing that man is a rational being in some measure, we cannot afford altogether to suppress their legitimate doubt by the name of some august being. When we want to prove the universality of a certain proposition, we find mere appealing to a power above us not so convincing and satisfactory as appealing to our own human nature or rationality. When we are told, "Say this, or do that, because it is in

accord with the inner reason of our being," we
feel more the nobility of human nature.

According to Buddhism, the question why we
must not discriminate between friends and foes
is answered by the doctrine of non-ego, as above
explained at some length. Therefore, the Buddhists declare: Regulate your thoughts and
deeds according to the feeling of oneness, and
you will find a most wondrous spiritual truth
driven home to your hearts. You are not necessarily thinking of the welfare and interest of
others, much less of your own; but, singularly
enough, what you aspire and practise is naturally
conducive to the promotion of the general happiness, of others as well as of yourselves. In such
an enlightened mind as has realized this most
homely and yet most ennobling truth, there is
no distinction to be made between friend and
enemy, lover and hater. He is filled with lovingkindness and brotherly-heartedness. And such
a one is called by Buddhists a Bodhisattva,
which translated means "intelligence-being," or
"one who has realized wisdom."

*   *   *

At this point we can turn to the positive
phase of Buddhism and ask ourselves what is
the doctrine that supplements the theory of
non-ego; for the latter is mainly concerned
with the destruction of the popular belief relating
to the nature of the ego, and, on that account,
it tends to emphasize the negative aspect of

Buddhism. We must have something positive when this erroneous belief is removed and be taught how to behave among the new surroundings into which we have thus been ushered. Most people are exceedingly alarmed when they are told that the self or the soul, which they cherished so fondly, is void in its nature, and will overwhelm us with a multitude of questions. To answer all these, however, is not my present purpose, as it will require a volume to satisfy those anxious truth-seekers. I wish only to say a few words here concerning the doctrine of Dharmakâya, which is the affirmative side of Buddhism.

Dharmakâya is a Sanskrit term, and it is very difficult to find a good English equivalent for it. *Dharma* means "doctrine," "law," "religion," "righteousness," "being," "essence," "norm," and such like; while *kâya* means "body," "organized being," "system," and so forth. Dharmakâya as a combined form of the two may be rendered "essence-body," "system of being," or "totality of existence." Whichever way we translate it, we find it very inadequate to express all that is contained in the original. In a word, it may be considered to be equivalent to the Christian conception of Godhead, and as such I will treat it in this discourse.

The Dharmakâya, however, differs from the Christian God, perhaps in its most essential aspects. Of course, even among Christians the

God-conception is subject to various interpre-
tations; and the Buddhist notion of Dharmakâya,
I venture to say, somewhat corresponds to the
Johannean view of God. Intelligent Christians,
I think, are well aware of the fact that the Gospel
of John strikes quite an independent key among
the Synoptics. Philosophically speaking, it rings
with a pantheistic note, while the other gospels
are monotheistic, true to the Jewish tradition.
Buddhism has a pantheistic tendency, too, and
in this respect the Gospel of John may be considered echoing somewhat the Buddhist sentiment.

Buddhists do not think that God has any
special abode, that his administration of the
universe comes from a certain fixed center or
headquarters, where he sits in his august throne
surrounded by angels and archangels and saints
and pious spirits who have been admitted there
through his grace. In short, the Buddhist God
is not above us, nor below us, but right in the
midst of us; and if we want to see him face to
face, we are able to find him in the lilies of the
field, in the fowls of the air, in the murmuring
mountain streams; we can trace his footsteps
in the sea, we can follow him as he rides upon
the storm; we can meet him in the bush; indeed,
wheresoever we may turn, we are sure to be
greeted by the smiling countenance of the author
of this universe. Who says, then, that God is in
Heaven, in some unknown region where we

mortals are never allowed to venture in without
his special permit?

This God of Buddhism works constantly and
everlastingly; he knows no rest, no fatigue, he
has not to stop his work after six days of toil;
he does not resort to any special revelation in
order to announce his existence to the world;
he has no favored son to sacrifice for the sake
of the sin of which the poor innocent child has
no conception. On the other hand, the Buddhist
God, is able to turn the meanest creature in the
world to the noblest figure in which his glory is
manifest to its full extent. He can destroy this
whole universe and raise it again in the twinkling
of an eye, it not being necessary for him to wait
even for three days. His revelation is not an
historical event, but it is happening every minute,
and those who have eyes see it, those who have
ears hear it. And to know the truth of this, it
is only necessary to cleanse the heart of its
egoistic impurities and defilements, which have
been accumulating by virtue of our subjective
ignorance. When this fundamental purification
is completed, "we all, with unveiled face reflect-
ing as in a mirror the glory of the Lord, are
transformed into the same image, from glory to
glory." Again, we are glorified with the "glory
which he had with him before the world was."
When we arrive at this exalted stage of spiritual
enlightenment, Buddhism declares that we have
attained Nirvâna. (Most Christian critics have

a very mistaken notion about the nature of Nirvâna, and this allusion is made with the view to clearing their minds.)

*   *   *

Supposing that I have made the Buddhist conception of God now somewhat intelligible to you, however broadly and sketchily, let me see what practical conclusion is drawn by the Buddhists from the above statement. If Buddhism teaches, as the Gospel of John declares, that "the Father is in me and I in him," or that "I and my Father are one," the practical ethics of Buddhism, it is evident, is to manifest the glory of God in all our conduct, in all our thoughts, in all our wishes and desires. It is evident, further, that as we are all one in God, his glory cannot be made manifest unless we break down the barrier of egoism which our ignorance and shortsightedness have built between mine and thine. Though this world, as it is, is manifesting the glory and love of God, the thought of selfishness which is so dearly cherished by our limited consciousness must be removed from the root, in order fully to appreciate the fact and truth. Buddhism does not exactly agree with Christianity when the latter emphasizes so much the distinction between the flesh and the spirit, as if they were altogether antagonistic to each other in their fundamental nature.

Buddhism, on the other hand, declares that all such distinctions as thine and mine, ego and God,

soul and flesh, "old man" and "new man,"
come from our own subjective ignorance, and
that when this darkness of nescience is eradi-
cated the flesh becomes at once the spirit, the
ego instantly assumes the aspect of the Holy
Ghost, as Christians would say. For from the
beginning there is neither flesh nor spirit, neither
"I" nor "thou," but the infinite intelligence
and love of the Dharmakâya. Therefore, Buddhists do not complain, "The spirit is willing,
and the flesh is weak"; but of the evil influence
of ignorance; and they concentrate all their
spiritual energy on the eradication of this ignorance and on the bringing about of enlightenment.
For enlightenment is Nirvâna; and herein the
doctrine of non-ego merges with the doctrine of
Dharmakâya.

* * *

I am not going here to draw a parallelism
between Buddhism and Christianity, nor to
present you a list of differences between the two:
I wish to give you in a summary way the main
points of the preceding discourse and conclude
this address. In a word, Buddhism is the
religion of enlightenment, in which the intellect
and the sentiment are harmoniously blended
together so as to realize the beatific state of
Nirvâna. Through the intellect Buddhists know
that there is no ego-soul which hides itself
snugly in the deepest recesses of the mind, that
the universe is the immanent expression of an

absolute, whence we come and whither we go, and that when we recognize negatively the unreality of the ego-monster we positively perceive the truth of the universal oneness of all sentient beings in the Body of Intelligence. While this is attained through the intellect, we come to feel through the objectives of the religious consciousness that the ultimate reality in which we live and move and have our being is not only intelligence but love—by love meaning the complete union and sameness of me and you.

Therefore, the Buddhist does not make it the purpose of his life to rise from the dead, to gain the immortality of a mythical being known as self, to lay up treasure for the future, to expect some reward in Heaven however spiritually that reward be considered, or to find consolation, to seek tranquillity of mind in relying upon some historical personage; but he endeavors to actualize the glory of God in this world while he is alive—the glory which he had before the world was—and which is made manifest only by following the way of God, by doing his will, that is, by practising in thought as well as in person the doctrine of non-ego, the precept of loving-kindness.

IMMORTALITY[1]

ONE of the many questions which I am very often requested to answer from the Buddhist point of view concerns the immortality of the soul. Thinking that this will also interest you, I wish to present my view on the question here.

It seems, everything depends upon the conception of the soul. Both you and I may use the same term, but if it is understood differently we cannot expect to come to any definite conclusion. I often think that if every notion, every concept, every sentiment we may happen to have, is so clearly defined as not to leave any point in obscurity, a great bulk of philosophical and religious controversy, which seems almost to make up the history of thought, will vanish. However this may be, let me first try to show you what I understand by the soul.

Buddhism uses the term Atman in place of soul and makes it signify that mysterious something which lurks in the background of our mental activities, and which soars up to an

[1]Read before Green Acre Fellowship, Washington, D. C., April, 1906.

unknown quarter usually known as heaven after
its departure from the body, within which it has
been imprisoned, and on which account it used
to long for liberation. The âtman or soul,
according to this conception, is not material,
exactly speaking, but something very much akin
to it, for it is an individual existence and therefore subject to the limitations of space and time
as well as to the law of causation. Though it
is impossible to think the soul other than material
if it is at all individual as conceived by ordinary
people, yet they make it at once spiritual and
individual—two qualities impossible to reconcile. Therefore, in point of fact, they materialize
the soul by their unwarranted—though pious
enough—attempt to make it immaterial and
spiritual. They are not indeed spiritualistic in
spite of their persistent claim to be so. They are
in fact materialistic. For if things are truly
spiritual and immaterial, in them there must be
the absence of all those qualities which make up
materiality, that is, they must not be bound by
the conditions of space and time. The existence
of a soul of this nature is most positively denied
by Buddhism. And those who aspire after its
immortality are designated ignorant, however
wise and intelligent they may be in affairs other
than religious.

It needs a certain amount of reflective power
to see in the popular conception of the soul a
grievous error which Buddhism endeavors to

remove. It may be more readily comprehended by the majority of people when we say that there is a mysterious metaphysical something in the mind which directs all its functions and operations according to its whimsical will, and which makes us believe in the reality of an ego-substance; than when we say that the so-called soul is no more than the unity of consciousness which is liable at any moment to dissolve, and which comes to exist when there is a certain co-ordination of all mental faculties. If you make the soul signify the notion which is popularly more intelligible, Buddhism will give you a very poor consolation, as it denies even the existence of such a shadowy object, not to speak of its continuance after the decay and dismemberment of the corporeal existence.

If this is found by you to be a little too abstract to be quite comprehensible, let me give you a favorite illustration frequently used by Buddhists to show the fallacy of belief in the existence of the soul. Do you think there is such a thing as the soul of the house who picks up the beams, roof, floor, walls, windows, etc., and puts them together in such a fashion as to make a house, and then hides himself in it somewhere, though altogether unrecognizable? Do you think again there is what is to be called the spirit of water who mixes up a certain amount of hydrogen with a portion of oxygen in order to make that most familiar and useful liquid and then convert

it into his own hiding-place? When the intellect
had not yet attained the present stage of development, people thought that there was in everything a spirit or a soul residing and living, and
who, when in wrath, found expression in raising
a tempest, in creating a hurricane, or in quaking
the foundation of the earth. But that time seems
to have departed forever.

A house is here when all the necessary things,
such as walls, pillars, beams, etc., are brought
together according to a certain form. Water
comes into existence when hydrogen and oxygen
combine themselves, each in a certain definite
percentage, according to their inherent constitution. It will be ridiculous, then, to imagine
that whenever we observe the waves stirring
or a mountain-stream rushing there is a soul in
the water who makes all these phenomena. The
conception of the human ego-soul is in perfect
parallel with that of the water soul-entity. If
waves, cataracts, whirlpools, or fountains are
possible without presuming the existence of a
water-ego, why do we hypostatize mentality
and conceive the ego as an ultimate reality?
Even scientifically speaking, this hypothesis does
not at all satisfactorily explain our mental
phenomena, but instead involves us in more
difficulties and complications. Accordingly, those
who hanker after the immortality of the soul
are said to be pursuing fata morgana which
vanish into airy nothingness as you approach.

Buddhism seems to be perfectly justified in declining to acknowledge the ego-soul.

What will then become of our innate desire after immortality? This is the question which will naturally come to you after you have followed me so far. To this I will answer: Seek that which is above birth and death, identify yourselves with it, and in that measure in which your identification is complete you will acquire immortality, and your religious sentiment will be thoroughly satisfied. Buddhism does not seek enlightenment in egoism, does not realize Nirvâna in the assertion of selfishness. Have your self-will removed and put in its place the divine will. "Not my will, but thy will," as Christians say, is that which is immortal in us, as well as that which constitutes the reason of our individual existences. As long as you have your selfish desires, impure motives, ignorant impulses, your immortality will never be gained. To be egoistic and to be immortal is to make "a" equal to "not-a," or to mix water with oil, as a Japanese saying goes; they exclude each other, and the result is unspeakable tribulation of spirit.

The problem of immortality has never troubled Buddhists, to speak frankly. When we were first asked about it, we did not know exactly how to grapple with it, for Buddhists are used to look at the matter from a totally different point of view. Their first effort is to comprehend the

whole, leaving the details behind. They first
want to grasp that which is changeless, is above
the transiency of phenomenality. When this is
accomplished, they find that they themselves
are part and parcel of that imperishable something. Though mortal as individual, particular
beings, they are a manifestation of the Great All,
and as such they will most assuredly survive all
forms of change and transformation. They have
then nothing to trouble themselves concerning soul
or no-soul and much less with its immortality.
All that they have ·to do is to come to a clear
consciousness of the reason of the universe and
to make its realization in them as perfect as they
can. Whether they live or not after the expiration of their physical lives does not concern them
at all. Let "thy will be done," and everything
else will run its own course, and are we not
relieved of the useless, wasteful worry and
anxiety?

If, in spite of all this, you feel somehow incon-
solable on account of nothing concrete surviving
after you but cold ashes and crumbling bones,
I would give you the immortality of work
(karma) instead of the immortality of the soul.
Or we might say that what you wish to understand by the soul does not exist in the ego-
entity but in the work you do, in the sentiment
you feel, in the thought you think, and if all these
are in accordance with "thy will" which disposes,
they will be what is left after you, that is to say,

you will forever live in them. When we stand before a canvas painted by a great painter, do we not feel the presence of the artist, as his ideas and feelings are embodied in it? Cannot we say that the artist is still living in his work? We do not know whether his soul has gone up to the heavens and is enjoying the celestial happiness, but we do know for certain that he is still living among ourselves and inspiring us to higher ideals of life.

Do you prefer the immortality of the soul as popularly understood to this kind of immortality that I have endeavored to expound here? If you do, I have nothing further to say, but that the immortality of work or deed or thought or sentiment seems to be more in accordance with the result of modern scientific investigation— not only that, but to be more satisfactory to our religious consciousness.

Before concluding, there is one thing I should like to ask the believers in a materialistic, individual soul and its immortality; that is, What do you want to do up in heaven when you are ushered in there after you have finished your earthly career? Is it your wish to sit quietly beside your Father and among the host of celestial beings and passively enjoy inexpressible blessings? If this is your wish for individual immortality, I fail to see the purpose and significance of this life on earth. The history of civilization seems to lose its purport when you are away from here.

Buddhists think otherwise than Christians in this respect. We consider our existence here below as a sort of link in the eternal chain of the divine revelation in the universe. We have not come on earth, each singly and separately, to assert only our individuality; but our fates are most solidly linked to our ancestors and their civilization as well as to our successors and their destiny. What we are to-day is due to the karma of our predecessors and at the same time will determine the fates of posterity. If we fail to enrich and ennoble our spiritual inheritance which originally came from the hand of the Dharmakâya, we entirely ignore the meaning of the history of humanity, we altogether disregard our responsibility to our forefathers and grand-children. We must not go to heaven and selfishly enjoy our individual immortality. On the contrary, we must abide where we are, and co-operate with one another for the ennoblement and enrichment of our earthly life. We must not be ungrateful for what our ancestors did for us, nor must we be inconsiderate of the welfare and enlightenment of coming generations. We must behave nobly, we must think rationally, we must feel unselfishly, and let us live in this karma which endureth forever, even after the dissolution of this physical existence.

Again, according to Buddhism, this universe is a sort of spiritual laboratory, in which all our ideal possibilities are experimented upon and developed and perfected. When this material garment wears out after a long use, we throw it away and put on a new one and appear in the same laboratory (and not anywhere else, not even in Heaven, let me remind you) as our own successors. We examine what our former lives have accomplished and apply all our moral and spiritual energy to the furtherance and perfection of the karma. The doctrine that the Buddha was able to reach his ideal eminence after his untiring practice of the six virtues of perfection (*pâramitâs*)[1] throughout his innumerable lives since the dawn of consciousness, is no more than the Buddhist conception of immortality and of the eternal striving after ideals. Let us, therefore, go not anywhere else after death even if an indulging benefactor should attempt to persuade us to join his celestial hosts; but let us remain in this universe, let the karma we have accumulated here bear its fruit and be brought to a happy consummation; for we are not strong enough to stand the grave charge to be preferred by posterity to the effect that we have scattered all our precious ancestral legacy to the four winds.

---

[1] (1) Charity, (2) Observation of Moral Precepts, (3) Meekness, (4) Energy, (5) Meditation, (6) Wisdom.

BUDDHIST FAITH.

BUDDHISM is so deep and comprehensive—
and, we might say, even unfathomable—that
scholars are sometimes at a loss how and where
to begin its measurement. In some respects it
appears to be a chaotic mass of superstitions,
while in others it is a systematic and thorough-
going application of an idealistic-pantheistic
theory. The present discourse does not propose,
however, to clear up all these difficulties, but only
to give a certain clue with which students of
Buddhism may be guided in their exploration.
Buddhism, then, will be treated here broadly
under two headings, Faith and Discipline.

First, of Buddhist faith, which is summed up
in this gâthâ:

"The Buddha-Body fills the world,
  Being immanent universally in all things;
  It will make itself manifest wherever and whenever
      conditions are matured,
  Though it never leaves this Seat of Bodhi."

Generally speaking, faith means trusting—
trusting in something external to oneself. When
religion is defined as a faith, it is considered to
imply that there is a being or power which has
created this world and presides over it, directing

its course and shaping its destiny; and that religion teaches to trust or believe in this being or power, which is thus proved to be greater and wiser than human beings. Therefore, Christians believe in a God who is a personal reality and who is supposed to exist above and outside of us poor mortals; and some Buddhists believe in Amitâbha Buddha, who resides in Pure Land or Western Paradise (*Sukhâvatî*); and for this reason religion has come to be identified with a belief in an external object, whatever this be, particularly by Occidental scholars. But Buddhist faith does not belong to this category, for Buddhism rejects the existence of a personal God as he is ordinarily understood by some religionists. What, then, is the faith that keeps Buddhists together?

Briefly, Buddhists believe in three most fundamental facts which are universally observable about us and which cannot be refuted by any amount of argument. They believe first in the sameness of things (*samatâ*). By sameness is understood the presence of a unifying principle in all phenomena. However diversified and differentiated may appear those particular existences with which we come in contact in this world of the senses, they universally partake of one nature, of one essence; and it is on account of this presence of a supra-individual reason that life becomes possible, that existence, this phenomenal world, becomes possible.

Secondly, Buddhists believe in the difference between things (*nânâtva*), in their manifoldness, in their particularity, in their individuality; for it is an undeniable fact that things are all separate and distinct, that each has its own individuality, that each moves according to its own inherent necessity.

Thirdly, Buddhists believe in the fact that all things move or work. For there is nothing in this world that is not endowed with the possibility of motion, the power of doing something, the capacity of accomplishing a work; and in exercising this power everything works upon another and is at the same time worked upon by another. The universe is a network of all these particular forces mutually acting and mutually being acted upon. This is called the principle of karma, and Buddhists apply it not only to the physical world but to the moral and spiritual realm.

This threefold faith constitutes the cornerstone of Buddhism, which makes it appear somewhat too metaphysical to be a religion of the masses, but the fact is that Buddhism is far from being a system of philosophy. Those who take Buddhists for speculative thinkers will lose sight of the inner life of the religion in which its followers are living. It must never be supposed that Buddhists try to get us entangled in the endless maze of sophistic reasoning. Anything that is to be designated at all as a religion never proposes to argue with us after the fashion of a philosopher; for religion is not to analyze, to demonstrate, or to argue with logical thoroughness, but to see facts directly and to believe and to live them accordingly.

In the gâthâ recited in the beginning, the idea of sameness is rather dogmatically expressed: "The Buddha-Body fills the world." In this the content of sameness is called Buddha-Body or in Sanskrit Buddhakâya. The Buddhakâya, which is also often called Dharmakâya, is the reason, life, and norm of all particular existences. When we penetrate through the diversity of all these individual phenomena, we encounter everywhere this indwelling Body and therein find the unity or sameness (samatâ) of things.

The principle of diversity is declared in the second line of the gâthâ, which makes the Buddha-Body universally immanent in all things. The Buddha-Body, the essence of existence, though absolutely one in itself, allows itself to be diversified as the lilies of the field, as the fowls of the air, as the creatures of the water, or as the inhabitants of the woods. For it is in the inherent nature of the Buddha-Body that it individualizes itself in the manifoldness of the phenomenal world. It does not stand alone outside particular existences, but it abides in them and animates them and makes them move freely. By thus abandoning its absolute transcendentality, it has subjected itself to certain conditions such as space, time, and causation. Its essence is infinite, but its manifestations are finite and limited. Therefore, the Buddha-Body has to wait to express itself in this relative world till all the necessary conditions are matured. This creation, so called, is no more than a manifestation of the self-limiting Buddha-Body.

Suppose here stands a mirror—the mirror of Buddha-Body. Anything that comes in front of it is reflected therein, and this without any premeditation on the part of the mirror. If there comes a man, he is reflected there; if a woman, she finds herself reflected in it; if it is a beautiful flower now which presents itself before the mirror, it is immediately and instantly reflected with all its magnificence. It is even so with things unsightly or even repugnant, for the mirror does not refuse its illuminating power to anything, high or low, rich or poor, ugly or beautiful, good or evil. Wherever and whenever conditions are ripe, all particular things will be reflected in the supra-natural mirror of Buddha-Body, without hesitation, without reasoning, without demonstration. This is the way in which the principle of karma works.

The fourth line of the gâthâ is more or less a continuation of the third and expresses the same sentiment from another point of view. Things are many, and are subject to constant transformation as regulated by their karma, but the

Buddha-Body eternally abides in the Seat of Bodhi, which is our inmost being.

The moon is one and serenely shines in the sky, but she will cast her shadow, wherever the conditions are mature, in ever so many different places. Do we not see her image wherever there is the least trace of water? It may be filthy, or it may be clean; it may consist of only a few drops, or it may be a vast expanse, such as the ocean; but they all reflect one and the same moon as best suited to their inherent nature. The shadows are as many as different bodies of water, but we cannot say that one shadow is different from another. However small the moon may appear when there is only a drop of water, she is essentially the same as the one in the boundless sheet of water, where its heavenly serenity inspires awe and reverence. So many, and yet one in all; so diverse, and yet essentially the same; we see it reflected everywhere, and yet is not the Buddha-Body sitting, all alone, in the Seat of Bodhi?

Several questions present themselves here: How can we attain a spiritual insight into the sameness of things, and have our minds so transparent as to reflect one eternal truth? How can we understand the principle of sameness in its phenomenal aspect and recognize it in the diversity of desires, feelings, passions, instincts, motives, etc.? How can we see the Buddha-Body in its manifold activities and recognize it at once without abstraction and premeditation and elaboration?

The most practical way to solve these problems is not through mere intellection. We must first acquire mental tranquillity, we must be purified spiritually, we must be freed from all disturbing passions, prejudices, and superstitions. Buddhism is a religion first and last, and its aim is always practical and spiritual. Philosophers and scientists will endeavor to come to a definite solution of the problems here cited logically, intellectually, metaphysically, analytically, relying on their demonstrative knowledge. But the way that leads us practical religionists most effectively to the satisfactory adjustment of the puzzling world-riddles which so greatly disturb all deep, serious souls is the practice of meditation, called Dhyâna[1] by Buddhists.

As to the practical part of Buddhism, or Discipline, it will be treated under "Buddhist Ethics," which follows.

[1]See the article "Practice of Dhyâna."   (See P. 146.]

BUDDHIST ETHICS

PAI LU-TIEN, a famous Chinese poet, author, and statesman who lived in the thirteenth century of the Christian era, once went to see an eminent Buddhist monk whose saintly life was known far and near, and asked him if he would instruct him in the essentials of Buddhist doctrine. The monk assented and recited the following gâtha:

> "Commit no wrong, but good deeds do,
> And let thy heart be pure,
> All Buddhas teach this truth,
> Which will for aye endure."[1]

The statesman-poet was not at all satisfied with this simple moral teaching, for he expected to have something abstruse, recondite, and highly philosophical from the mouth of such a prominent and virtuous personality. Said the poet, "Every child is familiar with this Buddhist injunction. What I wish to learn from you is the highest and most fundamental teaching of

---

[1] Translation by Dr. Paul Carus. In Pâli:
Sabbapâpassa akaranam, kusalassa upasampadâ,
Sacittapariyodapanam: etam Buddhâna sâsanam.
—Dhammapada, v. 183.

your faith." But the monk retorted, "Every
child may know of this gâthâ, but even a silvery-
haired man fails to put it into practice." Thereupon, it is said, the poet reverentially bowed
and went home meditatively.

If we are requested to-day to state what is the
most fundamental in Buddhist ethics, we have
to make the same assertion. There may be and
in fact are many schools and denominations in
Buddhism, each claiming to have transmitted
the true spirit of Buddha; but they will be
unanimous in declaring that the gâthâ afore-
mentioned is one of the common grounds on
which they all stand. "Sabba pâpassa akaranam" is heard in all Southern monasteries, and
the lines "Chu wo mo tso, etc.," are seen everywhere in the Eastern lands of Buddhism. If
Buddhism were called a sort of ethical culture
society on account of this simple code of morality,
its followers would make no objection to it, for
the recognition of a personal God, or the conception of original sin, or belief in a risen Christ is
not thought indispensable to Buddhist salvation.
Let a man do what is good and avoid what is bad
and have his heart as pure as he can of all egotistic
impulses and desires, and he will be delivered from
the clutches of ignorance and misery. Whatever his dogmatic views on religion, he is one
of the enlightened who are above bigotry, intolerance, vanity, conceit, pedantry, and prejudice.
He must truly be said to be one whose spiritual

insight has penetrated into the depths of existence.

Now, the question is: What is good? What is evil? And how is the heart to be cleansed? I am not going to discuss here these great ethical and religious problems from a mere theoretical point of view. Buddhism has nothing to do with utilitarianism or intuitionalism or hedonism or what not. Buddhism is most practical in its announcement of what constitutes goodness. It dogmatically and concretely points out good deeds one by one. First, negatively, it enumerates ten deeds of goodness (*kusalam*) as most fundamental in Buddhist ethics; while, positively, it considers the six pâramitâs (virtues of perfection) or eightfold path as the route leading to a virtuous life.

The ten deeds of goodness are: (1) Not to kill any living being; (2) Not to take anything that does not belong to oneself; (3) Not to look at the other sex with an unclean heart; (4) Not to speak falsehood; (5) Not to calumniate; (6) Not to use vile language; (7) Not to make sensational utterances; (8) Not to be greedy; (9) Not to be out of temper; and lastly, (10) Not to be confused by false doctrines. Later Buddhists, however, make ten affirmative propositions out of those just mentioned, thus: It is good (1) to save any living being, (2) to practise charity, (3) to be clean-minded, (4) to speak truth, (5) to promote friendship, (6) to talk softly and gently, (7) to be straightforward in speech, (8) to be content with one's own possessions, (9) to be meek and humble, and (10) to think clearly and rightly.

The six pâramitâs or virtues of perfection are: (1) Charity, which includes the giving away of worldly possessions as well as the proclamation of the Good Law, (2) The observation of the moral precepts as formulated by Buddha, (3) Meekness, (4) Strenuosity, (5) Contemplation, (6) Spiritual enlightenment.

The eightfold path is: (1) Right view, (2) Right reflection, (3) Right speech, (4) Right deed, (5) Right livelihood, (6) Right striving, (7) Right understanding, (8) Right contemplation.

In these various enumerations of Buddhist virtues, what is most unique are perhaps the virtues of strenuosity and those of contemplation and enlightenment. To be good Buddhists, we must never be indolent, whiling away our time to no purpose. Mere piety will not do, so long as there is some work to be accomplished for the sake of humanity and civilization. Love, again, must be accompanied with enlightenment, for the affection is very frequently wasted on account of its blindness. God-fearing is recommendable, but without contemplation we fail to recognize the purport of our own position in the system of the universe. Mere passion leads to fervor and violence if not properly guided by contemplation which brings enlightenment, revealing the reason of existence and purifying the heart of ignorance.

Ignorance, according to Buddhism, is the root of all evil, and therefore it advises us in strong terms to have ignorance completely destroyed. And it is only then that the all-illuminating light of enlightenment guides us gloriously to the destination of all beings, where we gain purity of heart, and whatever flows from this eternal fountain of purity is good.

It is evident, then, that by purity of heart is meant absence of ignorance and self-will. But it is not a negative condition, for the most essential postulate of Buddhism is that in each of us there abideth the indwelling reason of the universe, which, when released from the temporal bondage of ignorance and self-will, becomes the master of itself by reducing everything to subjection and restoring it to its right place. In a pure heart, therefore, the universal reason manifests itself in its full glory and works its own destiny unmolested. What one with such a heart wills is what makes the bird sing and the flower smile, what has raised the mountain and makes the water flow. He is hungry and the universe wishes to eat; he is asleep and all the world hybernates. This sounds extraordinary, but the enlightened understand it perfectly well. We cannot make the blind see what we ourselves see. The blind may protest that we are deceiving

them; but could we do otherwise, inasmuch as
they are deprived of the sense we have, or they
have not yet learned how to make use of it? It
is declared by Buddhists, therefore, that to
realize fully the sanctity of religious life one
must have Buddha-wisdom awakened from its
unconscious slumber in which it is indulging
from time out of mind.

Analytically, purity of heart consists of sympathy and intelligence, and on this groundwork
the structure of practical Buddhism is founded.
Sympathy is the tremulation of the spiritual
cord which unites the hearts of all sentient
beings; and it is intelligence that discovers the
presence of the sacred cord in every one of us
and keeps it from being entangled. The cord
freely responds to cries of suffering. The heart
contrives to effect all the possible means to
relieve sentient beings from misery and ignorance. The ten deeds of goodness, the eightfold
path, the six virtues of perfection, and many
other good things all flow from this one source
of pure-heartedness.

It is, then, of unqualified importance in the
ethics of Buddhism to have one's heart perfectly
cleansed and free from the dust of egotism
which has been accumulating through the want
of enlightenment. In this sense "blessed are the
pure in heart"; they may not see God as he is
superficially and superstitiously understood, but
they will surely come into personal touch with the

ultimate authority of conduct and also perceive that the author is not residing outside of their being but within themselves. We read in the *Dharmapada*:

"Manopubbangamâ dhammâ, manosetthâ, manomayâ;
 Manasâ ce padutthana bhâsati vâ karoti vâ,
 Tato nam dukkham anveti, cakkam va vahato padam.

"Manopubbangamâ dhammâ, manosetthâ, manomayâ;
 Manasâ ce pasannena bhâsati vâ karoti vâ,
 Tato nam sukham anveti, châyâ va anapâyinî."[1]

In this respect Buddhism can be said to have a decidedly idealistic tendency, since it fully recognizes the paramountcy of ideas in the moral realm. But we must not lose sight of the fact that Buddhism is not a system of metaphysics, but a religion which is practical more than anything else. What it teaches is the profound spiritual experience of every enlightened man, while the philosopher and theorist will speculate on the facts and offer whatever interpretation they may please or feel compelled to give to account adequately for them.

Buddhism is often charged with passiveness and quietism, lacking the "push" of some other religions; and the backwardness of Asiatic

---

[1] All that is, is the result of thought, it is founded on thought, it is made of thought. If a man speaks or acts with an evil thought, pain follows him, as the wheel follows the foot of the ox that draws the carriage. All that is, is the result of thought, it is founded on thought, it is made of thought. If a man speaks or acts with a pure thought, happiness follows him, like a shadow that never leaves him.

nations in the general march of humanity is sometimes ascribed to the influence of Buddhism. Though I am not here entering upon any lengthy polemics, a few words may not be altogether inopportune to refute such an erroneous opinion as this.

If there is anything passive in Eastern culture, which is often no more than tolerance or indifference or self-restraint, it is not due to Buddhism but to the racial idiosyncrasy of Asiatic peoples. Buddhism teaches contemplation and tranquillity and at the same time strenuosity, indefatigable energy in following truth and in destroying ignorance. We see many admirable examples among its believers who have fully illustrated these virtues in their person. The history of Buddhism, while perfectly free from bloodshed and inhumanity, evidences how far its moral teachings have been carried out. Buddhist ethics is not certainly passive or negative, unless the absence of arrogance, aggressiveness, intolerance, bigotry, and fanaticism could be called so.

Religion in its social aspect is not omnipotent, nor is it absolute, as is imagined by some. It is, like many other things created by man, a human institution; it has been discovered, shaped, developed according to the inner necessity of mankind; and as long as he is imperfect and steering his course through innumerable obstacles, religion also must share his imperfection and adapt itself to ever-changing surroundings. Instead of imposing its ideals upon man tyrannically and absolutely, religion reconciles itself to his needs, going through all the necessary modifications. Therefore, one religion is diversely interpreted by different peoples among whom it may thrive. To suppose that religion could do anything it desires without regard to individual, national, racial peculiarities is far from the fact. The difference between Oriental and Occidental civilization is by no means due to the difference between Christianity and Buddhism. On the other hand, the difference between the two religions is due to the difference between the two great types of civilization. Truth, be it religious or philosophical or scientific, is universal, and as such does not allow any modification or distortion. But it suffers modification in its practical application, for it is like a mathematical formula or figure. When conceived a priori, it is formal and not subject to any concrete individualization, which latter in fact is the condition of its particular forms.

In conclusion let me say most emphatically that the ethics of Buddhism is summed up in the purification of the heart, in keeping oneself unspotted even though living in the world; and from this eternal root must sprout such things of God as love, a heart of compassion, the virtue of strenuosity, humbleness of mind, longsuffering, forbearing one another, forgiving one another, and freedom from all evils.   It is said that there were eighty-four thousand virtues of perfection practised by all Bodhisattvas, but they are no more than so many leaves and branches growing from the one stem of pure-heartedness.

WHAT IS BUDDHISM?[1]

IT seems to be very appropriate and even necessary at the outset to draw a well-defined line of demarcation between what is understood as Hînayâna Buddhism and what is known as Mahâyâna Buddhism. Most people imagine that there is only one school of Buddhism and that that one school is no other than the Buddhism they have learned from the Buddhist books written or compiled or translated by Western Orientalists—Orientalists who are in many respects prejudiced against the doctrine which they propose to study most impartially. Owing to these unhappy circumstances, the outsiders are either generally ignorant or altogether misinformed of the true character of Buddhism. For what is understood by the Western people as Buddhism is no more than one of its main divisions, which only partially expresses the spirit of its founder.

I said here "divisions," but it may be more proper to say "stages of development." For Buddhism, like so many other religions, has gone

[1]Read before the National Geographic Society, Washington, D. C., April, 1906.

79

through several stages of development before it
has attained the present state of perfection among
the Oriental nations. And it will be evident to
you that if we catch only a glimpse of an object
and try to judge the whole from this transient
impression, we place ourselves in a most awkward
position, and shall be at a loss how to extricate
ourselves from it. Therefore, let me try in the
beginning to take a comprehensive view of the
subject we here propose to expound.

Properly speaking, Hînayâna Buddhism is a
phase of Mahâyâna Buddhism. The former is
preparatory for the latter. It is not final, but
merely a stepping stone which leads the walker
to the hall of perfect truth. Hînayânism is
therefore more or less pessimistic, ascetic, ethical
(to be distinguished from religious), and monas-
tical. It fails to give a complete satisfaction to
a man's religious yearnings. It does not fully
interpret the spirit of Buddha. The Buddhism
now prevailing in Ceylon, Burma, and Siam may
be considered to be betraying in a certain way
a Hînayâna tendency.

The Buddhism of present Japan, on the other
hand, is Mahâyânistic. It is more comprehensive, more religious, more humanistic, and more
satisfying to the innermost needs of the religious
consciousness. It cannot be said to be absolutely free from superstition, error, prejudice,
etc., for it is a constantly growing, ever-living
faith which knows no ossification or fossilization.

Some pious people are apt to consider their religious belief to be absolutely fixed and unchanging since the dawn of human consciousness; but they have forgotten, in my opinion, the fact that the human mind is still keeping on unfolding itself, that it has not yet exhausted all its possibilities, that it is constantly coming to a clearer consciousness as to its own nature, origin, and destiny. But what I firmly believe is that in the Buddhism of Japan to-day are epitomized all the essential results reached through the unfolding of the religious consciousness during the past twenty or thirty centuries of Oriental culture.

In a word, what has been known in the West as the teaching of Buddha does not represent it in its true, unadulterated color, for it is Hînayânistic in tendency; that is, it is exclusive and not comprehensive, narrow and limited, and not all absorbing and assimilating. What I propose to expound in this lecture to-night is the Mahâyâna Buddhism, so called by Buddhist scholars of the East.

Let me point out in this connection what is most characteristic of Buddhism as distinguished from any other religion. I refer to a predominant tendency of Buddhism toward intellectuality, and it seems to me that the reason why Buddhism is always ready to stand before the tribunal of science and let her pass a judgment upon its merits or demerits is due to this intellectual tenor.

It goes without saying that the intellect does not constitute the most essential element of religion, but we must not forget that a religious system too much given up to sentimentalism (understanding it in its purely psychological sense) is generally prone to accede to unwarranted mysticism, ignoring altogether the legitimate claim of the intellect. Buddhism is fortunately saved from this grievous blunder, and always endeavors not to give a free rein to the wantonness of imagination and the irrationality of affection. Love without enlightenment excludes, discriminates, and contradicts itself. Love is not love unless it is purified in the mill of spiritual insight and intellectual discrimination.

What are, then, the fundamental teachings of Buddhism? I deem it best to consider it from two standpoints, ethical and philosophical, or practical and speculative, or affective and intellectual. The philosophical or speculative is preparative for the ethical or practical, for religion is not a system of metaphysics which plays with verbalism and delights in sophistry, but its aim is pre-eminently practical and spiritual. It must bear fruit in this our everyday life.

To begin with the metaphysical side of Buddhism: (1) We Buddhists believe that as far as phenomenality goes, things that exist are all separate and discrete, they are subject to the law of individuation and therefore to that of

limitation also. All particular things exist in
time and space and move according to the law
of cause and effect, not only physically but
morally. Buddhism does not, though sometimes
understood by Western people to do so, advocate
the doctrine of emptiness or annihilation. It
most assuredly recognizes the multitudinousness
and reality of phenomena. This world as it is, is
real, not void. This life as we live it, is true,
and not a dream.

(2) We Buddhists believe that all these particular things surrounding us come from one
ultimate source which is all-powerful, all-knowing,
and all-loving. The world is the expression or
manifestation of this reason or spirit or life,
whatever you may designate it. However
diverse, therefore, things are, they all partake
of the nature of the ultimate being. Not only
sentient beings, but non-sentient beings, reflect
the glory of the Original Reason. Not only man
but even the lower animals and inorganic sub-
stances manifest the divinity of their source.
To use the Christian term, God, it[1] is visible
and audible not only in one of its highest manifestations, whom Christians call Jesus Christ,
but also in the meanest and most insignificant
piece of stone lying in a deserted field. God's

[1] Let me remark here that it is not at all proper to refer
to God, the ultimate source of everything, as masculine as
is usually done. God is above sex. It is neither "he"
nor "she." Even "it" is not appropriate, but will be prefer-
able to the other pronouns.

splendor is seen not only in the Biblical lilies, but also in the mud and mire from which they grow. The melody of divine reason is heard not only in the singing of a bird or in the composition of an inspired musician, but also in the "slums of life" as Emerson phrases it.

(3) This recognition of the oneness of things naturally leads to our third belief, that the one is the many and the many is the one. God does not dwell in the heavens. It does not direct its affairs in a closed office situated somewhere outside this world. It did not create heaven and earth out of nothingness. According to Buddhism, it is a serious error to seek God outside this life, outside this universe. It is living right among ourselves and directing the course of things according to its innate destiny. Though Buddhists refuse to have God walk out of us, they do not identify it with the totality of existence, they are not willing to cast their lot with pantheists so called. God is immanent, surely enough, but it is greater than the totality of things. For the world may pass away, the universe may be shaken out of its foundation, but God will remain and will create a new system out of the former ruins. The ashes of existence will never be scattered to the winds, but they will gather themselves in the ever designing hand of God and build themselves up to a new order of things, in which it is ever shining with its serene radiance.

To sum up the first part of this discourse, what may be called the metaphysical phase of Buddhism is to recognize (1) the reality of the phenomenal world, (2) the existence of one ultimate reason, and (3) the immanence of this reason in the universe.

Now to come to the practical side of Buddhism: The aim of Buddhism, to state it briefly, is to dispel the clouds of ignorance and to make shine the sun of enlightenment. We are selfish because we are ignorant as to the nature of self. We are addicted to the gratification of the passions, because we are ignorant as to the destiny of humanity. We are quarrelsome and want to make ourselves powerful and predominant at the expense of our fellow-beings, because we are ignorant of the ultimate reason of the universe. Buddhists do not recognize any original sin, but acknowledge the existence of ignorance, and insist on its total removal as the surest means of salvation. Let us, therefore, all be enlightened as to the statement made before. Let us know that we are all one in the reason of the universe, that the phenomenal world is real only to the extent it manifests reason, that egoism has no absolute sway in this life, for it destroys itself when it tries to preserve itself through its arrogant assertion, and that perfect peace is only attained when I recognize myself in you and you in me. Let us all be enlightened as to these things, and our ignorance and egoism are forever departed; the wall that divides is destroyed, and there is nothing which prevents us from loving our enemies; and the source of divine love is open in our hearts, the eternal current of sympathy has now found its unobstructed path. This is the reason why Buddhism is called the religion of enlightenment.

Now that we stand on this eminence of religious sanctity, we know what Buddhist practical faith is. It is threefold: (1) to cease from wrong-doing, (2) to promote goodness, and (3) to enlighten the ignorant. Buddhist ethics is the simplest thing to practise in the world. It has nothing mysterious, nothing superstitious, nothing idolatrous, nothing supernatural. Stop doing anything wrong, which is against the reason of things; do whatever is good, which advances the course of reason in this life; and finally help those who are still behind and weary of life to realize enlightenment: and here is Buddhism in a nutshell. It has nothing to do with prayer and worship and singing and what not. Our simple everyday life of love and sympathy is all that is needed to be a good Buddhist.

I was once asked whether there was such a thing as religious life particularly. To which my answer was simple enough: "Attend to your daily business, do all you can for the promotion of goodness in this world, and out of fulness of heart help your fellow-beings to gain the path of enlightenment. Outside of this there cannot be anything to be specially called a religious life."

In the latter part of the T'ang Dynasty in China, there was a famous poet-statesman who is known in Japanese as Hak-Rak-Ten. He learned that there resided in his district a Buddhist monk greatly noted for his saintly life and scholarly learning. The governor went to see him, intending to discuss some deeply religious topics. As soon as he was ushered into the presence of the monk, he inquired what was thought by the saint to be the most fundamental teaching of Buddhism. The monk immediately replied that it is the teaching of all enlightened ones to cease doing anything evil, to promote goodness, and to purify one's own heart.

Hak-Rak-Ten was nonplused to receive such a commonplace instruction from the mouth of such a scholarly personage professing the faith of Buddha; for he secretly expected to have something highly metaphysical and profoundly speculative, which would naturally lead them to further philosophizing and contentless abstraction. The poet-statesman therefore retorted: "This is what every child of three summers is familiar with. I desire on the other hand what is most abstruse, most essential, most vital in Buddhism." The monk, however, coldly replied: "Every child of three summers may know what I said now, but even a silvery-haired man of eighty winters finds it difficult to put the Buddhist instruction into the practice of everyday life."

And it is said that thereupon the Governor reverentially bowed and went home wiser.

What is philosophical in Buddhism is no more than a preliminary step toward what is practical in it. Every religion, if it deserves the name, must be essentially practical and conducive to the promotion of the general welfare and to the realization of Reason. Though intellectualism is 'one of the most characteristic features of Buddhism, making it so distinct from any other religious system, it never forgets the fact that our religious consciousness ever demands something concrete, that which is visible to our senses, that which is observable in our everyday life. Religion does not necessarily consist in talking on such subjects as the continuation after death of individual personality, original sin committed by some mythical personages, the last judgment to be given by an unknown quantity, a special historical revelation which takes place in a congested brain, and what not. At least, practical Buddhism does not trouble itself with solving these problems through speculation or imagination or sophistry. Let those theologians who delight in abstraction and supernaturalism discuss them to their hearts' content, for that is their profession. We, plain ordinary Buddhists, will keep on removing selfishness, seeking the light that is everywhere, practising lovingkindness that does not contradict or discriminate. Says an ancient sage, "The Way is near, and thou seekest it afar." Why, then, shall we ever attempt to walk away from the path which extends right in front of us, so wide and well paved?

THE MIDDLE WAY

HUNG JEN, the fifth patriarch of the Dhyâna sect in China, who died in 675 A. D., had many disciples. One day he made an announcement to them, saying that whoever was capable of giving a satisfactory proof of his thorough comprehension of Buddhism would succeed him in religious authority. And its outcome was the following two stanzas, the first by one of his most learned disciples and the second by his humble rice-pounder, who, however, was awarded the prize and came to be known later as the sixth patriarch.

> "The body is the holy Bodhi tree,
> The mind is like a mirror shining bright;
> Exert yourself to keep them always clean,
> And never let the dust accumulate."
>
> *   *   *
>
> "No holy tree exists as Bodhi known,
> No mirror shining bright is standing here;
> Since there is nothing from the very first,
> Where can the dust itself accumulate?"

*   *   *

The thesis I am going to expound this evening is that these two views of Buddhism must be reconciled and harmonized in order to walk on the middle path of truth. But before doing so let me acquaint you with the story of the blind men and the elephant.

There was once a powerful king in India, who called all his blind retainers together to his court, and then brought out one of his largest elephants before them, asking what they thought of it. Being born blind, of course they had never seen an elephant, and now in obedience to the royal command they all came around the animal. Each of them touched only a certain portion of the huge body and came to the hasty conclusion that the portion he handled was really the entirety of the beast.

Those that touched the tail thought the elephant was like a broom; those that touched the leg thought it resembled a huge column; those that touched the back imagined the elephant had a body with the shape of a gigantic drum; those that handled the ear thought it reminded them of the wing of a bird; those that touched the tusk thought it had the shape of a flail. Though thus none of them could describe the complete and exact figure of the elephant, each was narrow-minded enough to insist on the verity of his testimony. The king was very much amused to see how utterly they failed to comprehend the object and how fruitless their quarreling was.

Even so, says the Buddha, is the way most of us look at the truth and quarrel over it. Buddhists may think that Buddhism is the whole

truth and that all other religions are nothing
but superstition and prejudice; while Christians
will imagine that their religion is the only thing
in the world, that they are monopolizing the
divine grace, and that therefore all other teachings are impostures and idolatries and heathen-
isms. The adherents of Mohammedanism may
also be convinced of their absolute possession
of God; and so with all the other religious sys-
tems of the world. Indeed, every religion is
disposed to consider that it alone and no one
else holds the key to Heaven and eternal life;
and on account of this conviction religionists
are ever ready to denounce each other with
bitterness hardly worthy of their profession and
dignity. But to get at the real truth of things
we must shake off all these prejudices and
endeavor to comprehend the truth as a whole
and be always humble and broad-minded and
tolerant.

Now to return to the subject. These two
stanzas recited at the beginning are suited, I
believe, to illustrate in a way my point just
made; that is, to obtain a comprehensive view
of truth it is not enough to know only one side
of the shield, but we must turn it around and
see the reverse, as one is complementary to the
other. Judging superficially, the two stanzas
appear to be directly contradicting each other,
for while one advocates the strenuous life the
other seems to be tending to nihilism and liber-

tinism. In my opinion, however, Buddhism would be incomprehensible if these two apparently antagonizing views were not synthesized and harmoniously blended. To take hold of only one of these and to think that it comprises the whole of Buddhism will be committing the same error as the blind men in the story of the elephant.

Those two stanzas are the two wings of a bird, or the two wheels of a cart, or, perhaps more exactly, one is like the eye and the other the legs. With the eye we can see, but we cannot move, as we have no legs; with the legs we are able to move, but we are blind, as we are without sight. From the standpoint of absolute truth, there is no such thing as mind or matter or even God or universe. But if we confine ourselves to this view and become blind to the other side, which says that the many exists, that the world actually is, we are like the man who has no legs; we are unable to move, we cannot carry ourselves, we are helpless, we cannot live our daily life. Philosophical insight may be far-reaching enough, but it is contentless, it lacks the material on which to work. Therefore, we must look at the other side and see how our practical life is to be regulated; we must see how our legs are fixed, whether they are strong enough to take us where the eye is directing.

Again, we must not forget that practical discipline alone does not lead us to the abode of final enlightenment. It is very excellent not to neglect the cleaning of the mirror, the purifying of the mind, which is likely all the time to collect the dust of passion on it. But if we fail to see that a merely conventional, superficial purification is very much like groping in the dark without the knowledge of the import of existence, our spiritual horizon will draw itself within narrow limits like a snail retiring within the shell, and we may lose our original, intrinsic, spontaneous freedom and tranquillity, which belong to the mind by its own constitution; we may put ourselves under an unnecessary yoke, moving only within a prescribed circle. In other words, we may lose simplicity, naturalness, ease of movement in all our thinkings and doings.

In what follows I will consider the teaching of Buddhism as stated in those two stanzas harmoniously viewed.

The first stanza begins with the line, "The body is the holy Bodhi tree." In this, our body is compared to the sacredness of the Bodhi tree under which the founder of Buddhism attained his spiritual enlightenment and laid down the foundation of his system. The body, however evanescent in its character, must be considered holy even as the holy tree, and all the necessary care should be taken to keep it the worthy vessel in which the spirit is lodged. There are many fanatic believers in asceticism and self-mortification, thinking that this material existence is the root of evil and therefore the more is it tortured the purer and holier will grow the spirit. The flesh is in its very nature antagonistic to the spirit. They cannot thrive in harmonious relation with each other. The stronger the flesh the weaker the spirit, and vice versa. The line, "The body is the holy Bodhi tree," is directed against those who hold this kind of view. That is to say, Buddhism does not espouse any ascetic practice, nor does it hold a doctrine tending to a dualistic conception of existence which makes the flesh the source of evil and the spirit the foundation of everything good. The body as a material phenomenon has its limitations, as a living organism has its impulses, desires, passions, and moods; and there is nothing evil or wicked in it. It is thirsty and it must drink; it is hungry and it must be fed. Exposure in cold affects its well-being and it must be clothed. Too much strenuosity exhausts its energy and it must rest. All these things are inherent in it, and unless we demand that the tree grow as the fish, as a Japanese saying goes, it is altogether irrational to wish our bodily existence to be free from all its constitutional wants. Therefore, Buddhism teaches us not to curb them and torture the body, but to regulate them and prevent their going to self-destruction through wantonness.

The second line reads, "The mind is like a mirror shining bright." This may suggest, when contrasted with the first line, a dualistic con-

ception of our existence, making mind independent of body. But I am not going to
enter into this complicated problem,—the problem of mind and body, whether they are one or
separate. For convenience' sake, I take the
mind as the subjective aspect of the body and
the body as the objective aspect of the mind.
To speak more popularly, the mind is the inner
side of the body and the body the outer case of
the mind. They both make up one solid reality.
Within, it is felt as consciousness; without, it
is perceived as body. Now, this body is sacred
as the Bodhi tree, and every care has to be taken
for its well-being. So with the mind: it must
be kept perfectly free from the dirty particles
of passion, it must be made to retain its original
purity through moral discipline.

The mind as it first came from the hands of
God was pure, simple, illuminating as the mirror.
But in its constant contact with the world of
sense, it has become liable to be carried away
by its impressions and impulses without ever
reminding itself of its original immaculacy.
What comes from outside does not, of course,
defile the mind, but when the latter loses its own
control and gives way to sensuality, the dust
begins to accumulate on it. When its trans-
parency is thus gone, the mind becomes a play-
thing of all chance impulses and haphazard
impressions, like a river-ark drifting in the ocean
and being tossed up and down by the capricious

waves. Buddhism calls such a one ignorant and wanting in the Bodhi (wisdom). It therefore admonishes us to reflect within ourselves constantly and not to give a free rein to the sensual, selfish, unenlightened passions. The reason why Buddhism has so many moral precepts and monastic rules to regulate the lives of lay disciples and monks will now be understood. They are all intended for the purification of the mind and the regulation of bodily desires. They are all meant to ward off the evil influences that disturb serenity of mind and simplicity of heart, in order that our divine nature residing within us may fulfil its own significance and be free in its own operations. Buddhism does not desire to impede in any way our rational activities on account of those moral regulations, but simply to check the progress of evil desires, selfish impulses, and unenlightened motives.

So far we have dealt with the ethical and practical phase of Buddhism as enunciated in the first stanza. Now we must go round and see what is the other side of Buddhism, which constitutes the philosophical foundation of the system. It is not enough for us, it is not worthy of the name of a human being, merely to live and not to endeavor to unravel the mysteries of life. As a rational, conscious being, we must look into the reason of things, we must know the why of existence. To live even as a saint is not quite gratifying to the intellectual cravings of the human mind. Of course, every religion must find its culmination in our practical life and not in our abstract speculation. Yet we must seek a philosophical basis of conduct. And Buddhism finds this in the second stanza cited at the beginning of this discourse.

At the first blush the gâthâ seems to smack not a little of nihilism, as it apparently denies the existence of individuality. But those who stop short at this negative interpretation of it are not likely to grasp the deep signification of Buddhism. For Buddhism teaches in this gâthâ the existence of the highest reality that transcends the duality of body and mind as well as the limitations of time and space. Though this highest reality is the source of life, the ultimate reason of existence, and the norm of things multifarious and multitudinous, it has nothing particular in it, it cannot be designated by any determinative terms, it refuses to be expressed in the phraseology we use in our common parlance. Why? For it is an absolute unity, and there is nothing individual, particular, dualistic, and conditional. It is a great mistake, an intellectual weakness, to suppose that there is such a thing as a personal God or an immortal soul which stands like a mirror bright and shining and which is susceptible of contamination or corruption. For practical purposes we may provisionally admit the existence of an entity which some people call God and which is independent of this

world; we may again admit the existence of the
soul which is the master of this material phenomenon called body. But to understand these
things as actually existing as our short-sighted
intellect conceives them will be a fatal mistake.

We must first directly comprehend the spiritual reason of things, and then let us with this
insight look upon things that are about us. It
would be madness to deny the reality of the
phenomenal world, but in the midst of these
realities the enlightened see their non-reality.
There towers a huge mountain, here lies a boundless ocean, birds are singing, trees are growing,
and I sit here looking over the verdant meadow;
yet, in spite of all these, nay, indeed by reason of
these, I believe in the nothingness of existence,
in the non-reality of realities, and in the absolute oneness of all things; and it is thereby that I
gain my peace of mind and realize the sense of
perfect freedom in my everyday life.

All those moral laws and religious regulations
which I at first found unreasonably fettering my
free activity are now blessings, for I am no more
than those laws and rules themselves. I have
become master of them. I am the maker of all
those moral laws, and my existence consists in
the execution of them. I say this, my dear
Christian audience, and then ask you, "Does
your God feel himself hampered in his activity
when he has so many laws of nature to observe?
Does he, for instance, complain of the law of

gravity when he wants an apple to drop on the ground?'' Is he not perfectly free in following the laws of nature? and are we not made in his image? I see, then, no obstacles, no hampering, no discordant jarring in my following the laws of my being. And hereby we go back to the first stanza of moral discipline. We find now the middle course of truth, a complete harmonization of rigorism and naturalism, as the principles advocated by those two stanzas may respectively be so termed.

At first we had a feeling of compulsion and restraint, but now at the mastery of the second stanza we have philosophical intuition and feel perfectly at ease. We move as we will, yet we do not transgress. Our conduct, when our spiritual enlightenment reaches this stage, is in complete accord with the reason of heaven and earth, for we are now identified with it. From the start our religious discipline has been to attain this ease, this freedom, this simplicity, this spirituality, and we have at last reached the goal and are at rest. The bird has acquired two strong wings, the cart is supplied with a pair of running wheels, and we have the eyes that see and the legs that walk. There is nothing now in this life that will possibly cause vexation of spirit or the gnashing of teeth and the palpitation of heart.

THE WHEEL OF THE GOOD LAW

BUDDHISM is a religion which originated in India some five hundred years before the Christian Era. Its founder was Siddhartha Gautama, of royal lineage, who, becoming dissatisfied with the life he was born to enjoy, turned away from all forms of ease and luxury which surrounded him. He retired into the Himalaya Mountains when he was nineteen years old, or, according to another tradition, at the age of twenty-nine. He then devoted himself to penance and mortification, which was at the time considered a necessary discipline for those who sought wisdom and enlightenment. He visited many saints and philosophers whose virtue and wisdom were recognized by the people. Some years of rigorous ascetic life passed, and he was acknowledged by his religious comrades as their spiritual leader. But Gautama himself was not satisfied with this, because he was quite convinced that asceticism was not at all conducive to moral culture and spiritual enlightenment. He then altogether abandoned the practice of fasting and other modes of self-torture, and for taking this course of life he was deserted by his comrades. But his conviction and determination were not to be shaken by such trifling affairs; he kept on following what he thought would help him best to attain to wisdom and enlightenment.

After several years of deep meditation he awoke one morning under the Bodhi tree and most clearly perceived the way of enlightenment. He was now no more Gautama, a royal prince, but a Buddha, the enlightened one. He was so over-joyed with the revelation that he spent about a week most profoundly absorbed in contempla-tion, and it is even said that he was not at all inclined to come out of his transcendental ecstasy and self-reflection and to engage in active propa-ganda work in the world. But in the meantime his great compassionate heart asserted itself. His thought turned toward the miserable spir-itual conditions under which his former asso-ciates were laboring and from which he was now completely free. He went back to the woods where they were living. At first, they were disposed to deride their former leader, but as he approached his serene countenance and majestic demeanor completely unnerved them, and they prostrated themselves before him and asked his instruction. They were all converted to his view and came to enjoy the real bliss of life and enlightenment.

Buddha now thought of the world at large: "Though the masses are wretchedly struggling under delusion, prejudice, narrow-mindedness, bigotry, and superstition, there must be some in the world who are open to conviction, seeking the light of Dharma, Good Law, and those must be saved by all means. If they become enlightened, they will be able to perpetuate my teaching, posterity will learn through them of wisdom and enlightenment, and the truth will not be lost among sentient beings." Thus resolved, the Buddha came out into the world and made Deer Park in Central India the place of his first missionary activity. In describing this event, the Buddhists say that the Wheel of the Good Law, Dharmachakra, has been caused to revolve in this place for the first time in the history of mankind, marking the formal establishment of Buddhism.

The Buddha's long life of near ninety years consisted in never-tiring peregrinations along the banks of the Ganges and over the plains of Central India. He died while thus traveling, and there were present at the time only a few of his disciples surrounding his death-bed. His body was cremated and distributed among eight principal Buddhist kings of India who wished to honor their spiritual benefactor, each by erecting a splendid stupa or pagoda over his earthly remains.

*   *   *

Having thus roughly sketched the life of the founder of Buddhism, we ask now what is the

Wheel of the Good Law caused by him to revolve more than twenty-four centuries ago.

The most powerful motive that influenced Buddha, who was a royal prince, to abandon all his claims to the earthly advantages and to live a monkish, retiring, contemplative life, was his deep insight into the nature of life. He knew that life as it is lived by most of sentient beings was no more than a series of sufferings, for in trying to escape one misery they invariably fall into another misery which is perhaps greater and heavier to endure. He asked himself whether this misery could be exterminated. To ascertain this it was necessary to find out the real fundamental cause of it all. The removal of the cause was the removal of the effect.

In *Ignorance* he found the cause of misery that surrounds and oppresses us, sentient beings.

People are ignorant as to the real significance of existence; they blindly crave for it and its continuance merely for its own enjoyment; they do not know what destiny is awaiting them at the end of their earthly career; they do not know how pregnant of meaning is their every act, their every thought, their every feeling; they do not know under what conditions a phenomenon called life is possible, and finally they have a very confused notion concerning the true nature of the soul which they identify with the ego, simple, permanent, and absolute. On account of this ignorance, they suffer; on account of this ignorance, they keep on augmenting the causes of misery, and are unable to see the light of wisdom.

Buddha declares, there is no doubt that life is suffering, but it also affords enjoyment. The Buddhist life, however, is not to cling to either, for its real purpose is above the concatenation of pain and pleasure, sorrow and joy. Let us first be enlightened and not deviate from the path of righteousness, and we are saved.

The world in which we abide is a world of contrasts; the life we live is a life of opposites. We have the day and the night, we have the spring and the fall, we have men and women. Some are young, others are old; some are just breathing their last, others have now come to the world. The elements attract and repulse one another. The moon waxes and wanes. The waves are rising and receding. The stars are running toward one another and running away from one another. This is the world of constant change, of eternal motion, where takes place a never-ending interaction of forces. It is one force or one set of forces now that predominates, and then another. The point of concentration is eternally shifting. This is the actual experience of life and also its necessary condition.

Therefore, they will come inevitably to grief —they that disregard this experience and condition of life, they that seek in this world nothing but an everlasting continuation of pleasant,

agreeable sensations. They want to live, and
they do not know that their living is really their
death. This contradiction causes them an immeasurable amount of suffering. Apparently
they are living, that is, they are moving bodily
in the world of contrasts and opposites, of pleasures and pains, of sorrows and joys, of good and
evil; and yet they want to escape from this
actual state of things, they want to enter into a
region where they have only monotony, stag-
nation, and abeyance, and even extinction.
For are they not trying to keep the pendulum of
life always up on one side only? The pendulum
owes its existence to a constant swinging from
one side to the other. When this is stopped, it
ceases to be itself and exists no more. To live
is to move, to change, to walk up and down,
to come in and out, to enjoy and to suffer, to
smile and to weep. To refuse to do so is simply
courting death. Life is a fabric interwoven
with the woof of pain and the warp of pleasure.
It cannot be a monotonous series of pleasures,
nor that of pains. Therefore, to enjoy life is not
to crave for agreeable stimulations alone, nor is it
to shun evils. It is to be above them, both
pain and pleasure. It is to use the world, as not
abusing it, to state it from the Christian point
of view.

But many are they that are ignorant of this
our actual experience of life. How hard they
endeavor to create as much pleasure as they can

and to cling to it as long as they can, utterly
regardless of the true meaning of life! But it
is altogether outside of their power to check the
approaching shadow of misery which gradually
and stealthily but surely envelops them in the
end. The greater the joy of the moment, the
stronger its reverse. For where the mountains
are high, the seas are deep; and the blackness of
a raven looks blacker in the whiteness of snow.
It is therefore well to remind these hedonists of
the necessary condition of life, that there is no
pleasure that is not mingled with pain, that there
is no bliss which can be obtained without struggle.
Whatever blind pleasure-seekers think to be
bliss or curse is no other than the products of
sensualism and egoism, so long as they are
bound with the iron chain of ignorance. Their
deeds, sentiments, and thoughts have no moral
or religious significance whatever. Their lives
are like the bubbles or foam that vanish without
leaving any mark on the water. They die just
as they are born, blind, ignorant, and benighted.

Life, according to Buddhism, is worth living,
because it enables us to do something, because it
gives us a chance to work, to apply ourselves,
because it is the condition which makes possible
the realization of our moral and spiritual aspirations. Even if it is thought by some to be
worth living because it supplies us with pleasures
of passing moments or because it is desirable for
its own sake, Buddhists will not hesitate to sur-

render their lives once for all and will most
gladly be absorbed in the eternal abyss of death.
Life has nothing in itself worth clinging to, if
it did not promise us an opportunity to work.
As sentient, conscious beings that we are, it
would be most degrading in us to live the life
of a stone, to exist just for the sake of existence
and for no other purpose.

All conscientious Buddhists realize that there
are laws, natural as well as spiritual, in this
universe, and that those who dare to infringe
upon them are unerringly and even mercilessly
punished therefor. It does not make any difference that this infringement is unknowingly or
knowingly done, nor does it help the violator to
ask for a special grace. An evil act is committed,
and the universe is sorrowful for it, as it retards
so much the progress and realization of goodness.
But it will not let the evil-doer go unpunished.
Therefore, this existence has a purpose to attain,
an end to reach, an ideal to manifest; and all
beings animate and inanimate are working for
this universal goal. Our limited consciousness
may not have a very clear conception as to every
phase of the significance of life, but all enlightened minds are aware of this, that life is not for
mere living, but that it is the path which leads
to goodness, suchness, and oneness. The moral
and spiritual laws are instrumental for these
causes, and as long as we are moving in confor-
mity to the laws of conduct, we are promoting the

noble, worthy ideals, and our duties of life are thereby discharged. Pleasures and pains, joys and sorrows are merely accidents of life. They do not enter into its essential fabric. And consequently they are ignored by the Buddhists. They are not taken into any serious consideration in the determination or selection of duties of life.

Therefore, let us work, let us develop all our possibilities; not for ourselves, but for our fellow-creatures. Let us be enlightened in our efforts, let us strive after the general welfare of humanity and indeed of all creations. We are born here to do certain things. Life may be misery or not; it concerns us not; let us do what we have to do. We are not here wholly alone, we are not the center of the universe, everything is not coming to us. But our existence is conditioned. The fact that we are here at all is due to our mutual support and dependence. We cannot save ourselves unless others are saved. We cannot advance unless the general progress is assured. We must help one another, we must abandon our vulgar ego-centric ideas, we must expand ourselves so that the entire universe is identified with us, and so that our interests are those of humanity. It is therefore most evident that the assertion of the self-will and the giving way to the clamors of the ego-soul is against the reason of life. The attainment of Nirvâna and the manifestation of the Buddhist life is possible only through the denial of selfhood and through the united labor of all our brother creatures.

This is the doctrine proclaimed by the Buddha after many years of profound meditation on the bank of the Ganges, and constitutes the essence of the Wheel of the Good Law which has been in fact revolving ever since the dawn of sentiency.

The statements above made are usually put down in formula and called the Fourfold Noble Truth; viz., (1) Life is suffering, (2) There is cause for it, which is ignorance, (3) Nirvâna, which transcends pain and pleasure, is the goal of our life, and (4) To reach it the moral laws must be put into practice.[1]

---

[1]As for what is the practical ethics of Buddhism, read the article entitled "Buddhist Ethics." (P. 69.)

THE PHENOMENAL AND THE SUPRA-PHENOMENAL[1]

Aniccâ vata sankhâra,
Uppâdavaya dhammino;
Uppajjitvâ nirujjanti;
Tesam vûpasamo sukho.[2]

BEFORE entering upon an exposition of this stanza which I have selected for the subject of this morning's discourse, I wish to make a short preliminary remark concerning Buddhism generally.

In the study of Buddhism, one important thing which should be borne in mind by scholars is that the religion of Buddha has nothing to do with supernaturalism. Adhering to facts and their plain statements, Buddhists are always reluctant to give themselves away to personal authority or supernatural—which is, in fact, unnatural—revelation. Buddhism may therefore appear to some people rather flat, prosaic,

---

[1] A sermon delivererd at the Buddhist Mission of San Francisco, November, 1905.

[2] Translated into English:
Transitory, verily, are things,
Subject to law of birth and death;
Things born are doomed to die;
Their termination is bliss.

and unentertaining, lacking in the fertility and brilliancy of imagination—though this is by no means the case—and they call it sometimes a sort of ethical culture society and not a religious institution. For they think that no religion can exist without a belief in something extraordinary, miraculous, or supramundane which cannot be logically proved and individually experienced. But Buddha most emphatically insists that what he teaches is nothing unusual, being simply the recognition of a plain fact which can be attested by every mortal, that truth is not revealed to us from an unknown source, but is discovered by ourselves through the exercise of a faculty that can be acquired by all self-conscious beings, and that Buddhism is to be believed rationally and not blindly, to be believed because it is true and not because it has been proclaimed by some mythical personage. Whatever defects the teaching of Buddha may possess, I consider its rationality and matter-of-factness as one of its most characteristic and important features, distinguishing it from many another religion.

Further, this rationality of Buddhism is perhaps one of the many causes which make Buddhists remarkably tolerant and broad-minded toward their rival religionists. It is the pride of every conscientious Buddhist that the history of his faith is perfectly free from the stain of blood. When we of modern days turn over the pages of religious cruelty and barbarism, we are struck with a bitter sense of irony. It seems incredible that a religion proclaiming the gospel of love could practise such inhumanity. But I regret to say that even to-day there are some who are so hopelessly dogmatic and fanatical as to think that the rose could be sweet and fragrant only under its own name, that truth loses its worth and verity when known by any other name than their own, and that they would fight even unto death in order to replace one set of superstitions with another.

Science is steadily making its progress in various fields of human knowledge, and our intellectual sphere is being constantly widened; while pious, God-fearing religionists are still dreaming of the by-gone days, when their forefathers were engaged in the so-called holy wars, or when they were conducting the most atrocious, most diabolical outrage against humanity called the Inquisition. These facts often make me pause and think of their ultimate significance, wondering how slow man's progress is in things spiritual.

However this may be, Buddhism through its rationality and matter-of-fact-ness has never been intolerant and narrow-minded. It has always borne in mind that howsoever many avenues there may be to the summit of enlightenment, the position once gained will allow us all, regardless of racial and national variations, to see but one universal light of truth. The highest being is known under various names and appellations among various peoples on earth, according to their culture, education, and environment. Humanity, being essentially the same everywhere, it will sooner or later come to the knowledge of a supreme moral and spiritual power which governs the universe and whose commands we are compelled under penalty of annihilation to respect and obey. Whatever circumstances may lead to a difference of conception as to the details of its operation, the power of religion is fundamentally love,—love that does not exclude nor discriminate nor particularize; and this kind of love is realizable only when we recognize naturally and rationally and humanly the divinity of all existence and the universality of truth, in whatever divers aspects they may be considered and by whatever different paths they may be approached.

*   *   *

Now to return to the subject-proper of this discourse. Buddhism views the world under two aspects, phenomenal and supra-phenomenal. In the phenomenal world, the law of birth and death rules supreme, and here is nothing that will endure forever. Everything that exists under the sun is fleeting; it passes away as rapidly as the swift ships or as the eagle that swoopeth on the prey. The sun that has risen will set, the mountains so towering will crumble, the turbulent ocean will be drained, and the earth itself will be shaken from its foundations. That which has been is no more, and that which is is changing

fast.   Indeed, the world is no more than a constant flux of becoming.   Therefore, the Buddha
declares: "Transitory, verily, are things, subject to the law of birth and death; and things
born are doomed to die."

Mutability or impermanence is one of the most
universal facts of the world, and any one who
has his eyes wide open will certainly have to
recognize it.   And this recognition, when logically
carried out, will again certainly lead to non-
attachment; and non-attachment will in turn
bring out in us the desire for immortality.   The
reason why we cling to worldliness is because
we are not thoroughly acquainted with its true
character.   Its superficiality, its vainglory, its
illusiveness, its butterfly-like carelessness and
capriciousness,—all this seems to have a peculiar
fascination for the sensuous.   They have no time
to reflect deeply on the nature of these attrac-
tions, for they find themselves hopelessly involved
in the whirlpool of vanities before they can at all
think of extricating themselves therefrom.   They
look aghast at those who remind them of the
mutability of things and of the evanescent nature
of pleasures.

We can well imagine how desperate is the
situation of an undisciplined, unreflective mind
that almost mechanically pursues objects of sense
as the moth follows the flame.   But as soon as the
mind is awakened to the real state of the phenomenal world, it is unspeakably mortified at its

past folly and infatuation, and it will gradually develop the desire for non-attachment or freedom, in which it becomes estranged from its sensuous surroundings.

But can a mortal secure anything approaching eternity in this phenomenal realm? If everything here is subject to the irrefragable law of birth and death, we cannot in any way give satisfaction to our inner craving for things everlasting and immortal. Buddhism knows this our spiritual demand and teaches us that there exists a region which is supra-phenomenal and of which the spirit can drink to its satiety.

This supra-phenomenal world has no material limitations and therefore is not subject to the law of birth and death. As it is thus transcendent, it is beyond the reach of pain and pleasure, which is the pendulum that regulates the motive and conduct of the sensuous man. This latter is therefore unable to have even a glimpse of this heavenly region that lies beyond. He only who has freed himself from the shackle of phenomenality is no more affected by its mutability, and he is said to be living on the higher plane of existence. The mountains may be removed from their foundation, and the oceans may be exhausted, but a spiritual man will be above all such material vicissitudes, living a life of eternal peace. He calmly reviews the course of existence as it comes and disappears. He serenely abides in the realm of supra-phenomenality. He sees the lamp of eternity shining through the mist of transiency. He rises from the howling tempest of birth and death. Physically, he is, and will be no more, but spiritually he is living forever, unborn and imperishable. Because he has founded his kingdom in the Pure Land; where the waves of being and non-being beat no more; where the veil of ignorance and misery no longer hangs low; where the transitoriness of particulars is forever gone; where love, pure and infinite, embraces, absorbs, unifies every separate existence; and where joy inexpressible flows from the well of eternal peace. Therefore, the stanza above recited concludes with this line: "The termination of birth and death is bliss."

*   *   *

Now, the question again arises, Is this supra-phenomenal absolutely separated from the phenomenal world? If so, how can we of the latter ever expect or aspire to raise ourselves to the higher level of existence? If not, how can the supra-phenomenal be the phenomenal, and vice versa, seeing that they each have apparently irreconcilable characteristics? Learned Buddhist scholars will tell us how the identity of the supra-phenomenal and the phenomenal can be meta-physically established, and that our mental con-stitution demands this oneness, or, otherwise, a dualism, which inevitably results, will destroy the fundamental harmony of our logical reason-ing. But we who are aiming at the practical result of religious discipline would better eschew the theoretical part and be content with our inner individual experience. We would best avoid theorization and state the verdict of Buddhism on this problem rather dogmatically, which is: All depends upon our spiritual condition. If it is irreproachable and immaculate, supra-phenomenal is phenomenal, phenomenal is supra-phenomenal. Both are one and the same. Our earthly life is most exalted, most sacred, most divine, most religious. But if the spirit be defiled and corrupted, even a manifestly holy life is no more than gross blasphemy. All hinges on how we keep the spirit, pure or impure. Buddhism is thus thoroughly idealistic, as every true religion ought to be. It teaches the purification of the heart as the beginning and the end of all religious training.

Therefore, the heart holds the key which opens either the portal of sensuality or that of spirituality. In fact, these different portals do not exist objectively. The universe is one and the same for the just as well as for the unjust, but they approach it from various points of view and color it with their own inner pigment. Some are ignorant and selfish, and they interpret life accordingly. Others are simple-hearted and defilement-free, and thus they read the world. Conventionally, a distinction is made between the two worlds, supra-phenomenal and phenomenal, or sensual and spiritual, or worldly and saintly; in reality this is our own creation. Let us be free from delusion and sensualism, and things will present themselves in their own true color and form.

The termination of birth and death, pain and pleasure, desire and satisfaction, in short, of all sorts of dualism, does not mean to escape from the world and to lead an ascetic life, nor does it mean to commit suicide and put an end to existence, which is thought the root of all evil. Buddhism understands by the last line of the stanza recited at the beginning of this discourse the purification of the heart from all its selfish desires and defiled sentiments arising from ignorance and prejudice. For the self is no more than an illusory existence, and the separation of "me" from "thee" is fata morgana, and those who believe in their absolute reality are said to be confused. The heart essentially free and pure becomes contaminated as soon as it is caught in the meshes of egoism, and the result is the production of the three venomous desires[1] and the five consuming passions.[2] Of course, it would be madness to deny the relative reality of objects of the senses; no one can refute it. But if we go one step further and declare that their reality is final and ultimate, we logically put ourselves in the most awkward position and morally stand on the most unsteady ground. The irreconcilable egoism which char-

[1] Avarice, hatred, and infatuation.
[2] Inordinate desires arising from the five senses.

acterizes the life of the ordinary man is no more
than the natural outcome of this fatal realism.
To be saved, we must lift the veil of ignorance
and come out into the realm of "calm radiance,"
which is the abode of the enlightened.

The conclusion of the whole affair, then, is:
The world is characterized by mutability and
impermanence; those who do not rise above
worldliness are tossed up and down in the whirlpool of passion. But those who know the constitution of things see the infinite in the finite and
the supra-phenomenal in the phenomenal, and
are blessed in the midst of sufferings and tribulations.

REPLY TO A CHRISTIAN CRITIC

(LETTER WRITTEN IN 1896 TO DR. JOHN H. BARROWS.)[1]

DEAR SIR:

Friends in America have sent me a number of the *Chicago Tribune*, dated Monday, January 13, 1896, which contains the report of your second Haskell lecture, delivered at the Kent Theater in the Chicago University. The subject is "Christianity and Buddhism," and I anticipated a friendly and sympathetic treatment of Buddhism at your hands, for I do not doubt that you desire to be just in your judgment. Your utterances are of importance because they will be received as an impartial representation of our religion, since you, having been Chairman of the Religious Parliament, are commonly considered to have the best of information about those religions that were represented at this famous assemblage. I was greatly disappointed, however, seeing that you only repeat those errors which are common in the various Western books on Buddhism. You say, "The goal which made Buddha's teachings a dubious gospel, is Nirvâna, which involves the extinction of love and life,

---

[1] Reproduced from THE OPEN COURT, January, 1897.

as the going out of a flame which has nothing else to feed upon." Now the word *Nirvâna* means "extinction" and it means the eradication of all evil desires, of all passions, of all egotism, so that the flame of envy, hatred, and lust will have nothing to feed upon. This is the negative side of Nirvâna. The positive side of Nirvâna consists in the recognition of truth. The destruction of evil desires, of envy, hatred, extinction of selfishness implies charity, compassion with all suffering, and a love that is unbounded and infinite. Nirvâna means extinction of lust, not of love; extinction of evil, not of existence; of egotistic craving, not of life. The eradication of all that is evil in man's heart will set all his energies free for good deeds, and he is no genuine Buddhist who would not devote his life to active work, and a usefulness which would refuse neither his friends nor strangers, nor even his very enemies.

You say that "human life does not breathe, in Buddhism, the atmosphere of divine fatherhood, but groans under the dominion of inexorable and implacable laws." Now, I grant that Buddha taught the irrefragability of law, but this is a point in which, as in so many others, Buddha's teachings are in exact agreement with the doctrines of modern science. However, you ought to consider that while the law is irrefragable, no one but those who infringe upon it groan under it. He who understands the laws of existence, and especially the moral law that underlies the development of human society, will accommodate himself to it, and thus he will not groan under it, but in the measure that he is like Buddha he will be enlightened, he will be a master of the law and not a slave. In the same way that the ignorant savage is killed by the electric shock of lightning, while an electric engineer uses it for lighting the halls and streets of our cities, the immoral man suffers from the moral law, he groans under its inexorable and implacable decree, while the moral man enjoys it, and turning it to advantage glories in its boundless blessings.

This same moral law is the source of enlightenment and its recognition constitutes Buddhahood. This same moral law we call Dharmakâya, which is eternal, omnipresent, and all-glorious. We represent it under a picture of a father, and it was incarnated not only in Gautama-Buddha, but also in all great men in a higher or lesser degree, foremost among them in Jesus Christ, and, allow me to add, in George Washington, Abraham Lincoln, and other great men of your country. Allow me to add, too, that Buddha's doctrine, far from being skepticism, proclaims the doctrine that man *can* attain enlightenment and that he attains it not only through study and learning, which, as a matter of course, are indispensable, but also and mainly through *the earnest exertions of a life of purity and holiness*.

There are many more points in your lecture

which I feel tempted to discuss with you, but
they refer more to Christianity than to Buddhism,
and may imply a misunderstanding of Christian
doctrines on my part.   I am anxious to know all
that is good in Christianity and the significance
of your dogmas, so that I may grow in a comprehension of truth, but I have not as yet been
able to see that mankind can be benefited by
believing that Jesus Christ performed miracles.
I do not deny the miracles nor do I believe them;
I only claim that they are irrelevant.   The
beauty and the truth of many of Christ's sayings
fascinate me, but truth does not become clearer
by being pronounced by a man who works miracles.   You say that, "We can explain Buddha
without the miracles which later legends ascribe
to him, but we cannot explain Christ—either
his person or his influence—without granting the
truth of his own claim that he did the supernatural works of his father."   We may grant
that Jesus Christ is the greatest master and
teacher that appeared in the West after Buddha,
but the picture of Jesus Christ as we find it in the
Gospel is marred by the accounts of such miracles
as the great draft of fishes, which involves a great
and useless destruction of life (for we read that
the fishermen followed Jesus, leaving the fish
behind), and by the transformation of water
into wine at the marriage-feast at Cana.   Nor
has Jesus Christ attained to the calmness and
dignity of Buddha, for the passion of anger

overtook him in the temple, when he drove out with rope in hand those that bargained in the holy place.

How different would Buddha have behaved under similar conditions in the same place! Instead of whipping the evil-doers he would have converted them, for kind words strike deeper than the whip.

I do not dare to discuss the statements you make about Christianity, for fear that I may be mistaken, but I am open to conviction and willing to learn.

I hope you will not take offense at my frank remarks, but I feel that you, if any one in Christendom, ought to know the real teachings of Buddha, and we look to you as a leader who will make possible the way for a better understanding between all the religions of the world, for I do not doubt that as you unknowingly misrepresent the doctrines of the Tathâgata, so we may misunderstand the significance of Christianity. We shall be much obliged to you if in justice to the religion of Buddha you will make public this humble protest of mine, so that at least the most important misconceptions and prejudices that obtain among Christians may be removed.

I remain, with profound respect,

Your obedient servant,

Kamakura, Japan. SOYEN SHAKU.

IGNORANCE AND ENLIGHTENMENT.

THE fundamental idea of Buddhism is "to disperse the clouds of ignorance in order to make the moon of enlightenment shine out in her glory."

By ignorance Buddhism understands the assertion of self-will, which is the root of all evil and misery in this world. Self-will is ignorance, because it is blind to the truth that the world is a relative existence, that the self separated from other fellow-selves is non-entity, and that individuals acquire their reality in proportion as they penetrate the foundation of existence. This truth is ignored by the principle of self-assertion. A man who is self-assertive pushes himself forward without any regard to the welfare of his brother creatures; he hails himself when he reaches the heights of self-aggrandizement; but unfortunately he fails to perceive that his success is but the road to his final destruction. For self-assertion really means self-annihilation. We live in fact in the oneness of things and die in isolation and singleness.

In Christian terminology, selfhood is the "flesh," or "the old man"; such is the meaning when Jesus exclaims that "the spirit is truly ready, but the flesh is weak" (Mark xiv, 38), or when Paul speaks of "the old man which is corrupt according to the deceitful lusts" (Eph. iv, 22), or when the flesh is spoken of as profiting nothing (John vi, 63), or allusion is made to its infirmity (Rom. vi, 19), or to its not pleasing God (Rom. viii, 8), or to its lusting against the spirit (Gal. v, 17). Christians are not so intellectual as Buddhists, and therefore, philosophically considered, the terminology of the former is not so definite and to the point as is that of the latter. Besides, the adoption of popular terms often suggests a wrong conception which is not intended; for instance, the distinction between the flesh and the spirit has a tendency to a dualistic interpretation of life. To conceive the nature of the flesh to be diametrically and radically opposed to that of the spirit is not in accord with the essentially monistic teaching of Buddhism. Those who are prone to asceticism and self-mortification are as much condemned by Buddha as the followers of hedonism for being ignorant and far from attaining the path of enlightenment.

When the ignorance of self-assertion is removed, Buddhism teaches, the enlightenment of universal lovingkindness takes its place; and the arrogance, tenacity, indefatigability, and impertinence which characterize egotistic impulses are all converted to do service for the general welfare of humanity,

and they will then assume different names as
most desirable virtues. As soon as the veil of
ignorance is raised, the glory of enlightenment
which is love is revealed, and we do no more
hanker after self-gratification. Why? Because
the Buddha-intelligence is universal and works
in every one of us to bring out the consciousness
of oneness underlying all individual phenomena.
We as individuals are all different; mine is not
thine and vice versa; and in this sense egoism
is true, and the assertion of self-will is permis-
sible to that extent. But we must never lose
sight of "the same God that worketh all in all,"
and "in which we move and live and have our
being," for he is the source of eternal life and the
fountain of love. "Not what I will, but what
thou wilt," is the most fundamental religious
truth, not only in Christianity, but in Buddhism.
Not the assertion of self-will, but the execution
of the will of that being in which we are all one,
constitutes the condition of enlightenment.

We must not, however, suppose that the
divine will becomes manifest only when all the
lust and passions of the flesh are destroyed.
This is the teaching of anchorites and not of
Buddhists. What the latter teach is to make
the inclinations of the flesh those of the spirit,
so that there will be left no hiatus between the
two. What one wills, the other wills, and no
discord or mutual exclusion is then allowed. To
express this more Buddhistically, ignorance does

not depart when enlightenment comes in, but
ignorance itself becomes enlightenment; self-will
is not annihilated in order to make room for the
divine will, but self-will itself assumes divinity.

In the beginning of this discourse, I said that
the fundamental idea of Buddhism is to disperse
the clouds of ignorance in order to see the moon
of enlightenment in her glory. This may suggest the thought that ignorance and enlightenment are fundamentally different and mutually
contradicting, and that one thing called ignorance goes out and another thing called enlightenment comes in to take its place, as these two
do not agree. But in truth I have there followed
the popular dualistic conception of the matter;
and therefore let me repeat that in Nirvâna,
according to Buddhism, there is not such distinction as light and shade, ignorance and enlightenment, coming and going. If there is anything
in Nirvâna, it is all enlightenment, all purity,
and an unconditioned freedom from selfishness.
Accordingly, when one attains Nirvâna, which
is the realization of the Buddhist life, ignorance
itself becomes enlightenment and self-will the
divine will. What we thought ignorance is now
enlightenment; where we located the final abode
of the ego-soul, we have now the fount of divine
will. This may sound somewhat sacrilegious,
but the Buddhists are such consistent and never-
yielding monists that they do not shrink from
carrying out their logic to the end; they are not

at all afraid of the charge of blasphemy or irre-
ligiosity likely to be preferred by some pious
Christians.

This purification or illumination of self-will,
however, must not be confused with antinomi-
anism or libertinism.   The latter is given up to
the wantonness of self-will and not to the free
activity of the divine will.   What the pure-hearted
do is always pure, while whatever comes from a
heart defiled with egoism is defiled and irrational.
There are many points in the religious life which
make it very difficult to distinguish the latter
from the ethical life, for both are so closely related.
But we could consider the subjectivity of religion
as most characteristically contrasted to the
objectivity of ethics.   The distinction between
the self-will and the divine will must be personally
felt and individually experienced.   This may
sound vague and be considered as taking refuge
in the maze of subjectivism; but the fact is that
religion has its foundation in our subjective life,
and anything that relates to it lacks in definition
and exactitude so typical of things objective and
intellectual.   Religion, when devoid of this
mystical element, loses its irresistible fascination.
Of course, we must not make it abide always in
the camera obscura of imagination and mysticism.   We must take it out in the broad daylight
of science and subject it to an intellectual scru-
tiny.   But we cannot for all that ignore the fact
that there is something in religion which defies

or escapes the most penetrating searchlight of intellectual analysis. And in this something there lies its charm, its raison d'etre, and its power to remove vexation of spirit.

Whatever this be, Nirvâna, in which the spirituality of a human being is fully realized, can be attained only after most strenuous moral efforts on the part of the aspirant. Intellectual knowledge can be acquired through an outside agency; we of latter days may be far wiser in this particular respect than all our venerable moral and religious teachers of bygone ages, such as Socrates, Plato, Buddha, and Christ. But the spiritual region lies within, and each of us must strive, through our own inner and individual efforts and not through any outside agency, to unfold ourselves and bring about enlightenment. We may have high ideals, but let us remember that they can be realized only after long discipline and untiring exertion. Let those therefore forever strive—those that wish to follow the fundamental idea of Buddhism.

"When the scholar driveth away sloth by earnestness,
    He attaineth to the palace of wisdom,
    Sorrowless in the sorrowing world,
    And the wise one, he, looks upon the ignorant,
    Even as one on the mountain-peak looks upon one on
        the ground."   —Dharmapada, 28.

SPIRITUAL ENLIGHTENMENT

THERE are many characteristic points of divergence between religion and philosophy, though they have so much in common that some scholars, broadly speaking, take religion for practical philosophy and philosophy for speculative religion. The difference between the two, however, is not merely that of practicability and theorization. It is, in my judgment, more deeply rooted and fundamental. What is it, then? I believe that that which makes religion what it is in contradistinction to philosophy or ethics consists in the truth that it is essentially founded on facts of one's own spiritual experience, which is beyond intellectual demonstrability and which opens a finite mind to the light of universal effulgence. In short, spiritual enlightenment is indispensable in religion, while philosophy is mere intellection.

By spiritual enlightenment I mean a man's becoming conscious through personal experience of the ultimate nature of his inner being. This insight breaks as it were the wall of intellectual limitation and brings us to a region which has been hitherto concealed from our view. The horizon is now so widened as to enable our spiritual vision to survey the totality of existence. As long as we groped in the darkness of ignorance, we could not go beyond the threshold of individuation; we could not recognize the presence of a light whose most penetrating rays reveal all the mysteries of nature and mind. The spirit has found that the light is shining within itself even in its fullest glory, that it even partakes something of this universal light, that it blundered miserably in seeking its own ground outside of itself, that "Alpha and Omega, the beginning and the end, which is, and which was, and which is to come," is no more nor less than itself. And it is through this kind of enlightenment only that we fully satisfy our inmost spiritual yearnings and groanings. Without this, religion loses its significance, becoming merely an applied philosophy or system of metaphysics.

The enlightenment which thus constitutes the basis of the religious life is altogether spiritual and not intellectual. The intellect in its very nature is relative and cannot transcend its own limitations. It is dualistic no matter how high it may take a flight. It always needs an object with which to deal, and it never identifies itself with it, for it cannot do so without destroying itself. There must be the "I" and the "not-I" whenever intellection takes place. Self-alienation or keeping itself aloof from the object on which it exercises itself is the raison d'etre of intellect, being its strongest as well as its weakest point. Its strongest point is seen in science and philosophy, while its weakest point is revealed in religion. For religion needs a synthetic faculty by which it can comprehend the realm of particulars, the realm of constant strivings and eternal contradictions. Religion wants to understand and preserve life as it is found, and not to "dissect and murder" it as is done by the intellect. Religion wants to see and not to demonstrate; to grasp directly with her own hands and not to rely upon a medium; to see intuitively and not discursively. What is therefore asked for by a religious spirit is fact and not representation, enlightenment and not reflection; and this will be supplied by no amount of speculation and imagination. We must advance one step further beyond the limits and boldly plunge into the abysmal depths of the Unknowable.

Can a mortal being with his limited consciousness have an insight into a field without its ken? No; as long as he relies solely upon his intellectual faculty, he is forever barred from so doing. For the intellect is really superficial and cannot penetrate through spatial and temporal relations, nor can she free herself from the bondage of logical sequence; and therefore the inner life of our being is altogether unknown to the intellect. We cannot be said to know an object thoroughly by merely becoming familiar with all its attributes, qualities, potentialities, and what not.

All these can be understood through the senses
and the reasoning faculty. There yet remains
a certain feature of the object, the knowledge
of which alone completes our understanding of it.
Philosophy and science have done a great deal
for the advancement of our knowledge of the
universe, and there is a fair prospect of their
further service for this end. But they are con-
stitutionally incapable of giving rest, bliss, joy,
and faith to a troubled spirit; for they do not
provide us with a complete knowledge of éxist-
ence, and are unable to lay bare the secrets of
life. . What they teach concerns the shell and
husk of reality. In order to satisfy fully our
religious yearnings we must not stop short at
this; we must appeal to a different faculty, which
will reveal to us the inmost life of the universe.

Fortunately, we are in possession of this peculiar
faculty which might be called the religious sense,
and through the exercise of which we come to
realize the significance of our existence. How
unbearable life would be, if we were not allowed
to have this religious faculty and yet we had to
raise those spirit-harassing questions which could
not be solved by logic!

The faculty seems to have all the essential
characteristics of the feeling. It is intuitive and
does not analyze; it is direct and refuses a
medium of any form. It allows no argument, it
merely states, and its statement is absolute.
When it says "yes," the affirmation has such a

convincing force as to remove all doubts, and
even skeptically disposed intellectual minds have
to admit it as a fact and not a whim.   It speaks
as one with authority.   True, it has only a subjective value, which, however, is just as ultimate
and actual as sense-perception.   Being immediate,
there is no other way to test its validity than
that each experience it personally, individually,
and inwardly.   The sun is risen on the horizon
and all that have eyes see it and harbor not the
shadow of a doubt as to its presence there.   The
inner sense which I have called religious faculty
makes us feel the inmost life that is running
through every vein and every artery of nature;
and we are completely free from skepticism,
unrest, dissatisfaction, and vexation of spirit.
We never try to raise a doubt about the true
nature of the feeling and ask ourselves whether
it is merely a phenomenon of mental aberration
or due to a calenture of the brain.   We simply
feel, and nothing more or less is to be asserted
or denied.   And this is what constitutes spiritual
enlightenment.

Mere talking about or mere believing in the
existence of God and his infinite love is nonsense
as far as religion is concerned.   Talking and
arguing belong to philosophy, and believing in its
ordinary sense is a sort of hypothesis, not necessarily supported by facts.   Religion, however,
wants above everything else solid facts and
actual personal experience.   If God exists, he

must be felt. If he is love, it must be experienced and become the fact of one's inmost life. Without spiritual enlightenment, all is an idle talk, like a bubble which vanishes under the least pressure. Without the awakening of the religious sense or faculty, God is a shadow, the soul a ghost, and life a dream. In Buddhism this faculty is known as *Prajnâ*.

If we distinguish faith from knowledge, the latter can be understood as simply intellectual, while the former is intuition gained through the exercise of the Prajñâ. In knowledge subject and object coexist and condition each other; in faith they become one, there is identity only and no mutuality. Transcending the reciprocity of the "I" and the "not-I," the Prajñâ beholds the universe in its ultimate oneness and feels all forms of life in their essential sameness. It knows that the impulse it feels is the quickening spirit of all existence, and that the pulsation of sympathy which beats in response to outside stimuli is the source of universal animation. Why? Because the Prajñâ feels so by reason of its own constitution.

The dictates of the Prajñâ are final and there is no higher faculty in our consciousness to annul them. Faith is absolute within its own limits and the office of the intellect is to explain or interpret it objectively. Speaking religiously, faith is fact and has to be reckoned with as such. It is only when it wants to express itself that intellection comes in, and individual culture or personal equation makes itself felt. To a great extent, I feel that differences or quarrels among the so-called religionists concerning their confession of faith are due to personal differences in esthetic taste, intellectual calibre, and the influence of environment, while the fact of faith as such remains fundamentally the same with Christians, Buddhists, or Taoists. As everybody endowed with sentiency feels the ice cold and the fire warm, so what the Prajñâ sees or feels in its inmost being must be universally the same. God, Allah, Dharmakâya, Tao, Holy Ghost, Brahma, and what not, are a mere verbal quibbling over the same fact which is felt in the deepest depths of our being. The inner reason of things which creates or destroys the three thousand worlds in the same breath must be smiling at the human trifling over naught.

Spiritual enlightenment must not be confused with trance, a state of consciousness in which there is nothing but blankness. Those who have had no spiritual experience or who have not come to recognize in the awakening of Prajñâ something altogether unique in our subjective life-phenomena frequently speak of enlightenment as an abnormal psychical condition, and try to explain it under the same category as hallucination, somnambulism, self-suggestion, and the like. But the fact is that enlightenment is not a special psychic state which excludes or suppresses the ordinary exercise of other mental faculties. Enlightenment goes and must go along with all psychological phenomena. If enlightenment is to be gained through the suspension of mentation, religion is false and faith is barren. Enlightenment is enlightenment because it enlightens all our motives, desires, whims, determinations, impulses, thoughts, etc. It does not stand separate from other states of consciousness, sending its commands from a certain vantage ground. In an enlightened mind a feeling or thought as it occurs is purified and free from the taints of ignorance and egotism. Enlightenment is constant and not sporadic. It permeates every mental fibre and works without rest. It is not something extraordinary that takes place by fits and starts. Spiritual enlightenment sheds light on the very reason of consciousness, for it is not a particular event of our psychical life.

When a Buddhist scholar was asked what was the Path, he answered, "The normal state of mind." In other words, spiritual enlightenment consists in following the natural course of human activity, for the enlightened find the ultimate reason of existence in their desire to drink or to eat according to their natural appetite, in their sympathy for the misery and suffering which are endured by the ignorant masses, in their aspiration to fathom the mysteries of nature and life, in their ever-assiduous attempt to realize the

ideals of lovingkindness and universal brotherhood on this earth, in their ever-varying devices
to let each creation fulfill its inherent mission
and rest in its reason of existence. The religiously ignorant behave outwardly just as the
enlightened, for as far as intellect and morals
go there is no manifested difference between the
ignorant and the enlightened. But, spiritually
speaking, there is a wide gap dividing them,
because one knows what he is striving after while
the other is blindly feeling his way, and again
because one finds an unspeakable bliss in all
his doings and thinkings and feelings, while the
other labors under a peculiar sensation of
uneasiness and compulsion which he cannot well
define but feels at the bottom of his heart.

A person may be very learned in all things,
and his philosophical knowledge may be very
profound. He has studied all the ancient lore
of wisdom, and has even formulated his own
system of metaphysics in which he has incorporated all the results of his erudition and speculation. But from the religious point of view
he is yet far from enlightenment, for his study
is like that of the artist who has painted a dragon
and forgot to put the eyes in. His elaborate
delineation and coloring in various hues of this
huge mystic animal have miserably failed to
produce the effect desired and attempted, for the
eyes are blank and show no trace of the fiery
animation which is possessed by the monster.
The scholar has neglected the most important

factor that is absolutely necessary in making
up the complete knowledge of the universe. He
thought that he knew everything under the sun
when he exercised his intellectual power to its
full extent and considered existence from all the
possible standpoints which his understanding
could grasp. But, as I stated before, the knowledge of an object is not complete unless its inner
life or reason is felt; in other words, unless the
duality of a knowing mind and a known object
vanishes, and life is comprehended as it is and
not in its intellectual mutilation. Buddhism says
that even a blade of grass trembling in the evening breeze cannot be known so long as we cling
to this form of individuation and are unable to
merge our particular selves with the self of
grass. Buddha, it is reported, once brought a
flower before an assemblage of his disciples and
showed it to them without any comments whatever, and the entire congregation was bewildered
what to make of this strange behavior on the
part of their master, except Kâshyapa, who,
thoroughly understanding the import of this
incident, softly smiled and nodded. Thereupon
the Buddha solemnly proclaimed, "I am in
possession of the Eye which penetrates into the
depths of the Dharma and the mysteries of
Nirvâna. I now give it to thee, O Kâshyapa,
that thou mayest guard it well." What sort of
eye could it have been which was transmitted
from Buddha to Kâshyapa and which made the

latter comprehend something incomprehensible in the flower in Buddha's hand?

In this we see the discrepancy between philosophy and religion more and more accentuated. It is sufficient for philosophy to know, but religion demands more than that. When the existence or non-existence of God is *proved*, philosophers are satisfied, for they have made the utmost use of the intellect, which is their sole weapon of attack and defense. In fact, they sometimes show a disposition to deride those who disagree with them. But as long as there is some unutterable yearning in the human heart for something more real, more vital, more tangible than mere abstraction, mere knowing, and mere "proving," we must conclude that our consciousness, however fractional, is capable of coming in touch with the inmost life of things in another way than intellection. The existence of Prajñâ, the organ of spiritual insight, therefore, is admitted by Buddhism, and their religious discipline is directed towards the awakening of this faculty, which is rightly designated "the mother of all Buddhas," and "the sharpest sword that cuts ignorance and egotism."

But one must not imagine that there is consciousness, there is Prajñâ, and there is enlightenment. In point of fact, they are all one simultaneous act of the universal reason. We speak of them as if they were three different things: the sentient being is endowed with consciousness, and this consciousness has the faculty to become acquainted with its own reason of existence, and the resultant mental state constitutes what is called spiritual enlightenment. Intellectually, this distinction of course is inevitable, but as a man actually experiences it, the only fact he is conscious of is that he is, not as a particular being separate from others, but as simply existing and living. Buddhist scholars call this exalted state of spirituality *çûnyatâ* = emptiness, or *çânti* = tranquillity, or *samâdhi* = contemplation.

A few words may not be amiss here to explain these terms, which have been frequently misunderstood by the outsider. "Emptiness" may suggest a deprivation of all mental operations as in the trance, and "tranquillity" a dormant, sleeping, or "not-yet-awakened" state of mentality, while "contemplation" tends to indicate a withdrawal or suspension of all psychical functions; thus making spiritual enlightenment a synonym of death or annihilation. Such misinterpretations as these, however, ever prove the inherent onesidedness of the understanding and consequently its inability to lead us to the final abode of eternal reason which has really "no-abode." Buddhists use the term "emptiness" to describe the "deep things of God" which are absolute and not relative. For when we say, "he is," it may be taken as meaning that he is as we individuals are.

By "All is empty, quiet, and abiding in eternal

contemplation," Buddhists understand that the ultimate reason of the universe as manifested in all forms of animation and intelligence knows no disturbance, no commotion, no transgression, in the midst of all the stirring-up and moving-on of this phenomenal world. This, again, I have to state, guarding against misapprehension, does not mean that there is something within each existence which like the axle of a wheel or like the kernel of a seed forms its central part and remains quiet or alive even when the peripheral parts are whirling around or going to decay. Buddhism most emphatically condemns this sort of dualism as heretical and evil-breeding. The ultimate reason is absolutely quiet when it is moving on; it is perfectly empty when it is filled to the brim; it is eternally one when it is differentiating itself into myriads; it has no abode whatever where it finds itself located, housed, and roomed. And there is nothing paradoxical or enigmatic in this statement; it is plain as daylight and simple as the logical axiom $a = a$. But to realize its truth one must be spiritually enlightened, must go beyond the narrow limits of intellection, must drink directly from the well of eternal vitality and find out personally how it tastes, bitter or sweet.

Let philosophers and theologians say whatever they wish concerning the existence, nature, and activity of God; let them speculate as much as they wish on the theology of the universe and the destiny of mankind and many other abstruse problems of metaphysics; but let you who earnestly aspire to know what this life really means turn away from those wise men and reflect within, or look around yourselves with an open heart which watches and receives, and all the mysteries of the world will be revealed to you in the awakening of your Prajñâ.

PRACTICE OF DHYANA

THREE things are usually considered necessary for the realization of the Buddhist life: 1. *Çîla* (moral precepts), 2, *Dhyâna* (contemplation), 3, *Prajnâ* (wisdom); and these are coöperative and mutually related.

To be a good Buddhist, first of all, a man must be ethical and regulate his life according to the moral precepts, which were laid down by Buddha and are universally applicable. Next, he must be philosophical, that is, he must train his mind so as to be capable of practising introspection. The mechanical observance of the moral laws is not becoming to the dignity of a rational, conscious being. Man must be master of himself, intellectually, morally, and spiritually. To be so, he must be able to examine his own states of consciousness and direct his thoughts and desires to the end where lies the rationale of existence. This habit of self-examination is attainable only through the practice of dhyâna, contemplation. Lastly, he must be religious, by which is meant that he should have an insight going deep into the indwelling reason of things, and this insight, according to Buddhism, is the outcome of the mental training acquired by self-introspection. Prajñâ, which is the most fundamental of all the psychic faculties possessed by man, lies inactive and altogether unrecognized when the mind is busily engaged in receiving impressions and elaborating on them through the ordinary process of understanding. It has no time to withdraw within itself and watch how impulses are awakened, stimuli felt, thoughts matured, in short, how the inner working goes on. It never knows what a precious stone it harbors within its being, which, when discovered, will illuminate the inmost significance of life and put an end to all vanities and vexations of spirit. The practice of dhyâna, however, brings this latent faculty of consciousness to the surface and makes a new man out of old, worn-out, and apparently unpromising stuff.

Therefore, the three requisites of the Buddhist life are helping one another like a tripod to stand together and to accomplish their common purpose. The moral precepts cannot be intelligently and thoroughly followed unless a man has gained a complete control of himself through contemplation and self-introspection. But this dhyâna-practice will not be of much value, religiously considered, to his daily life unless it leads to the awakening of Prajñâ (wisdom) and to the comprehension of the ultimate facts of life. Whatever difference there may be in the different schools of Buddhism, those three forms of discipline, as they are often called, are admitted by them all as most essential for the realization of their ideal life. The importance of the moral codes as formulated by Buddha will not be questioned even by followers of non-Buddhist faiths, and as to the signification of spiritual insight, which constitutes the essence of religious life, I have somewhere touched upon the subject. In this short discourse I wish to say a few words concerning the practice of dhyâna.

*   *   *

Dhyâna is essentially Hindu or, rather broadly speaking, Oriental in its origin as well as in its significance. In this we can trace one of the many characteristics which lend a peculiarly charming color to Oriental culture. The Oriental mind ever strives after the One and is so idealistic in all its tendencies as sometimes altogether to ignore the external world. It shuts out all the impressions the senses may bring in from without, thus endeavoring to realize the aspiration after unity and eternality. It does not care so much for the subjugation of natural forces to its own will as for the deliverance of self from its illusory imprisonment. It does not antagonize the world in which it lives, but calmly contemplates it, reviewing its vagaries or vicissitudes, or whatever they may be termed. It dwelleth not in the manyness of things, but in their oneness, for its ultimate abode is in the region of the absolute and not in the phenomenal realm.

A mind like this naturally takes more to contemplation than to the strenuous life; it thinks more and acts less; it appreciates instead of criticizing; it synthesizes instead of analyzing. The practice of dhyâna, therefore, was the most natural thing for the Oriental people.

The Western people were not altogether unfamiliar with dhyâna, as we can judge from the life of a mystic or a medieval Christian monk. But their so-called contemplation or meditation was not as systematic and did not necessarily form a part of their religious discipline. The Hebrews were too fanatically religious to allow themselves the time to reflect. The Greeks were rather scientific and intellectual, while the Romans were pre-eminently practical. The German mystics perhaps were more or less after the Hindu type in their general mental constitution, but they seem not to have made the practice of dhyâna a prominent feature of their doctrine. Be that as it may, there is no doubt that dhyâna is an Oriental production

What is dhyâna, then? Dhyâna literally means, in Sanskrit, pacification, equilibration, or tranquillization, but as religious discipline it is rather self-examination or introspection. It is not necessarily to cogitate on the deep subjects of metaphysics, nor is it to contemplate on the virtues of a deity, or on the transitoriness of mundane life. To define its import in Buddhism, roughly and practically, it is the habit of with-

drawing occasionally from the turbulence of
worldliness and of devoting some time to a quiet
inspection of one's own consciousness. When
this habit is thoroughly established, a man can
keep serenity of mind and cheerfulness of disposition even in the midst of his whirlwind-like
course of daily life. Dhyâna is then a discipline
in tranquillization. It aims at giving to a mind
the time for deliberation and saving it from
running wild; it directs the vain and vulgar to
the path of earnestness and reality; it makes
us feel interest in higher things which are above
the senses; it discovers the presence in us of
a spiritual faculty which bridges the chasm
between the finite and the infinite; and it finally
delivers us from the bondage and torture of
ignorance, safely leading us to the other shore
of Nirvâna.

Dhyâna is sometimes made a synonym for
çamatha and samâdhi and samâpatti. Çamatha
is tranquillity and practically the same as
dhyâna, though the latter is much more frequently
in use than the former. Samâpatti literally is
"put together evenly" or "balanced," and means
the equilibrium of consciousness in which takes
place neither wakefulness nor apathy, but in
which the mind is calmly concentrated on the
thought under consideration. Samâdhi is a perfect absorption, voluntary or involuntary, of
thought into the object of contemplation. A
mind is sometimes said to be in a state of

samâdhi when it identifies itself with the ultimate
reason of existence and is only conscious of the
unification. In this case, dhyâna is the method
or process that brings us finally to samâdhi.

*   *   *

Now, the benefits arising from the exercise of
dhyâna are more than one, and are not only
practical but moral and spiritual. Nobody will
deny the most practical advantage gained through
presence of mind, moderation of temper, control
of feelings, and mastery of oneself. A passion
may be so violent at the time of its agitation
that it will fairly consume itself to utter destruction, but a cool-headed man knows well how to
give it the necessary psychological time of rest
and deliberation and thus to save himself from
plunging headlong into the Charybdis of emotion.
And this cool-headedness, though in some measure due to heredity, is attainable through the
exercise of dhyâna.

Intellectually, dhyâna will keep the head clear
and transparent and, whenever necessary, make
it concentrate itself on the subject at issue.
Logical accuracy depends greatly on the dispas-
sionateness of the arguing mind, and scientific
investigation gains much from the steadiness of
the observing eye. Whatever be a man's intellectual development, he has surely nothing to
lose, but a great deal to gain, by training himself in the habit of tranquillization.

In these days of industrial and commercial

civilization, the multitudes of people have very little time to devote themselves to spiritual culture. They are not altogether ignorant of the existence of things which are of permanent value, but their minds are so engrossed in details of everyday life that they find it extremely difficult to avoid their constant obtrusion. Even when they retire from their routine work at night, they are bent on something exciting which will tax their already over-stretched nervous system to the utmost. If they do not die prematurely, they become nervous wrecks. They seem not to know the blessings of relaxation. They seem to be unable to live within themselves and find there the source of eternal cheerfulness. Life is for them more or less a heavy burden and their task consists in the carrying of the burden. The gospel of dhyâna, therefore, must prove to them a heaven-sent boon when they conscientiously practise it.

Dhyâna is physiologically the accumulation of nervous energy; it is a sort of spiritual storage battery in which an enormous amount of latent force is sealed,—a force which will, whenever demand is made, manifest itself with tremendous potency. A mind trained in dhyâna will never waste its energy, causing its untimely exhaustion. It may appear at times, when superficially observed, dull, uninteresting, and dreamy, but it will work wonders when the occasion arises; while a mind ordinarily addicted to dissipation

succumbs to the intensity of an impulse or a
stimulus without much struggling, which ends in
complete collapse, for it has no energy in reserve.
Here, let me remark incidentally, can be seen
one of the many characteristic differences between
Orientalism and Occidentalism. In all depart-
ments of Oriental culture a strong emphasis is
placed upon the necessity of preserving the
latent nervous energy and of keeping the source
of spiritual strength well fed and nourished.
Young minds are trained to store up within and
not to make any wasteful display of their prowess
and knowledge and virtue. It is only shallow
waters, they would say, that make a noisy, rest-
less stream, while a deep whirlpool goes on
silently. The Occidentals, as far as I can judge,
seem to be fond of making a full display of their
possessions with the frankness of a child; and they
are prone to a strenuous and dissipating life
which will soon drain all the nervous force at
their command. They seem not to keep anything in reserve which they can make use of later
on at their leisure. They are indeed candid
and open-hearted—traits which sometimes seem
wanting in the Orientals. But they certainly
lack the unfathomableness of the latter, who never
seem to be enthusiastic, clamorous, or irrepres-
sible. The teaching of Lao-tze or that of the
Bhagavadgîta was not surely intended for the
Western nations. Of course, there are exceptions
in the West as well as in the East. Generally

speaking, however, the West is energetic, and the East mystical; for the latter's ideal is to be incomprehensible, immeasurable, and undemonstrative even as an absolute being itself. And the practice of dhyâna may be considered in a way one of the methods of realizing this ideal.

*   *   *

In the *Chandradîpa-samâdhi Sûtra*, the benefits of dhyâna-practice are enumerated as follows: (1) When a man practises dhyâna according to the regulation, all his senses become calm and serene, and, without knowing it on his part, he begins to enjoy the habit. (2) Lovingkindness will take possession of his heart, which, then freeing itself from sinfulness, looks upon all sentient beings as his brothers and sisters. (3) Such poisonous and harassing passions as anger, infatuation, avarice, etc., gradually retire from the field of consciousness. (4) Having a close watch over all the senses, dhyâna guards them against the intrusion of evils. (5) Being pure in heart and serene in disposition, the practiser of dhyâna feels no inordinate appetite in lower passions. (6) The mind being concentrated on higher thoughts, all sorts of temptation and attachment and egotism are kept away. (7) Though he well knows the emptiness of vanity, he does not fall into the snare of nihilism. (8) However entangling the nets of birth and death, he is well aware of the way to deliverance therefrom. (9) Having fathomed the deepest depths of the Dharma, he abides in the wisdom of Buddha. (10) As he is not disturbed by any temptation, he feels like an eagle that, having escaped from imprisonment, freely wings his flight through the air.

*   *   *

The practice of dhyâna is often confounded with a trance or self-hypnotism,—a grave error which I here propose to refute. The difference between the two is patent to every clear-sighted mind, for a trance is a pathological disturbance of consciousness, while dhyâna is a perfectly normal state of it. Trance is a kind of self-illusion which is entirely subjective and cannot be objectively verified, but dhyâna is a state of consciousness in which all mental powers are kept in equilibrium so that no one thought or faculty is made predominant over others. It is like the pacification of turbulent waters by pouring oil over them: no waves are roaring, no foams are boiling, no splashes are spattering, but a smooth, glossy mirror of immense dimension. And it is in this perfect mirror of consciousness that myriads of reflections, as it were, come and go without ever disturbing its serenity. In trances certain mental and physiological functions are unduly accelerated, while others are kept altogether in abeyance, the whole system of consciousness thus being thrown into disorder; and its outcome is the loss of equilibrium in the organism—which is very

opposite to what is attained through the practice
of dhyâna.

Again, some superficial critics think that
Buddhist dhyâna is a sort of intense meditation
on some highly abstracted thoughts, and that
the concentration which works in the same way
as self-hypnotism leads the mind to the state
of a trance, called Nirvâna. This is a very
grievous error committed by those who have
never comprehended the essence of religious consciousness, for Buddhist dhyâna has nothing to
do with abstraction or hypnotization. What it
proposes to accomplish is to make our consciousness realize the inner reason of the universe
which abides in our minds. Dhyâna strives to
make us acquainted with the most concrete and
withal the most universal fact of life. It is the
philosopher's business to deal with dry, lifeless,
uninteresting generalizations. Buddhists are not
concerned with things like that. They want to
see the fact directly and not through the medium
of philosophical abstractions. There may be a
god who created heaven and earth, or there may
not; we could be saved by simply believing in
his goodness, or we could not; the destination
of evil-doers may be hell and that of good men
paradise, or this may be reversed: true Buddhists
do not trouble themselves with such propositions
as these. Let them well alone; Buddhists are
not so idle and superficial as to waste their time
in pondering over the questions which have no

vital concern with our religious life. Buddhists through dhyâna endeavor to reach the bottom of things and there to grasp with their own hands the very life of the universe, which makes the sun rise in the morning, makes the bird cheerfully sing in the balmy spring breeze, and also makes the biped called man hunger for love, righteousness, liberty, truth, and goodness. In dhyâna, therefore, there is nothing abstract, nothing dry as a bone and cold as a corpse, but all animation, all activity, and eternal revelation.

Some Hindu philosophers, however, seem to have considered hallucinations and self-suggested states of mind as real and the attainment of them as the aim of dhyâna practice. Their conception of the eightfold dhyâna-heaven in which all sorts of angels are living is evidence of it. When the mythical beings in those regions practise dhyâna, they enter into different stages of samâdhi. They first come to think that they are lifted up in the air like a cloud; (2) they feel the presence of some indescribable luminosity; (3) they experience a supernatural joy; (4) their minds become so clarified and transparent as to reflect all the worlds like a very brilliant mirror; (5) they feel as if the soul has escaped bodily confinement and expanded itself to the immensity of space; (6) they now come back to a definite state of consciousness in which all mental functions are presented and the past and present and future reveal themselves; (7)

they then have the feeling of absolute nothingness, in which not a ripple of mentation stirs;
(8) lastly, they are not conscious of anything
particular, nor have they lost consciousness,
and here they are said to have reached the
highest stage of samâdhi.

But according to Buddhism all these visionary
phenomena as the outcome of dhyâna are rejected,
for they have nothing to do with the realization
of the religious life. In the *Çûrangâma Sûtra*
fifty abnormal conditions of consciousness are
mentioned against which the practiser of dhyâna
has to guard himself, and among them we find
those psychical aberrations mentioned above.

*   *   *

To conclude. Dhyâna, beside its being an
indispensable religious discipline for attaining
enlightenment, is one of the most efficient means
of training oneself morally and physically. It
is beyond question that dhyâna leads to the
awakening of a hidden spiritual faculty possessed by all conscious beings and to the realization of one's spiritual significance in spite of
the various material limitations. But, apart
from this religious importance, dhyâna is singularly effective in the tranquillization of the
mind, the purification of the heart, as well as
in the relaxation of the nervous tension. A
man will never realize, until he is thoroughly
trained in dhyâna, how confused and entangled
his thoughts are, how susceptible he is and how

easily his mind is unbalanced, how soon his nervous force in reserve is exhausted and his entire system is given up to an utter breakdown, how fully his senses are occupied in seeking excitement and gratification, and finally how neglectful he has been in the promotion of higher and nobler interests of life and in the cultivation of refined thoughts and purer feelings. Dhyâna, therefore, whatever its religious merits, is not devoid of its practical utilities and even for this reason alone its exercise is universally to be recommended.

KWANNON BOSATZ

THE topic of my discourse to-day is Kwannon Bosatz, or Goddess of Mercy as she is commonly known.

I am not going, let it be remarked at the beginning, to make any historical investigation of this deity, or Bodhisattva according to Buddhist terminology. I am not concerned here with the pedigree of Kwannon, who was originally a Hindu male deity of greatest energy, called Avalokiteshvara. Whatever history she may have had in ancient India, the deity is no more known to us as she or he was. According to our present knowledge, Kwannon has come to be identified with his consort Târâ and is no longer a male deity representing supreme energy, but as the goddess of mercy and love, the principle of universal lovingkindness. We shall take her, then, as we understand her in these latter days, ignoring altogether her historical development. Moreover, Kwannon is no more a Hindu deity, but has completely been naturalized in the Far Eastern soil.

In my opinion, man's religious needs are essentially the same whether he has his accidental place of birth in the East or in the West. When he feels the needs, he endeavors to find the best means of gratification according as he is situated, either in his history or tradition or folklore or superstitious beliefs. From the material thus obtained he constructs the real thing needed, and with his intellectual development he elaborates it and brings it to perfection. When we see this finished production of man's inner religious yearnings, we altogether put aside its historical relations and appreciate it as it is as a manifestation of man's inner nature. Our consideration of Kwannon will then be from this standpoint.

Now, Kwannon consists of two words, *kwan* and *on*, which is an abbreviation of a fuller title, Kwan-ze-on. *Kwan* literally means "to see," "to perceive," or "to look upon." But let me remind you that this perception is not physical, not sensorial, but spiritual, inward, and transcendental. It is an insight into the true significance of things with the mental eye which is possessed by all sentient beings. The next character, *ze*, means the "world" or "universe," including everything that exists; and the last, *on*, is "sound" or "voice." Taken altogether, Kwan-ze-on is "one who perceives the world-sound."

Here I have to remark that the sound Kwannon perceives, it may be known to you, is not physical, that it has no reference to the wave-motion of atmosphere, which reaching our audi-

tory nerves is interpreted as sound. When we
view things that are about us with the spiritual
eye, they all become convertible to one another,
so that one can be expressed by the terms of
another: sound is color, color is taste, odor is
sound, etc. From the sensuous point of view,
this is altogether incomprehensible, for what the
eye sees is color and what the ears hear is sound,
and they are absolutely irreducible to each other's
terms. In the phenomenal world individuation
rules, and things cannot be otherwise than they
appear to our particularizing senses. But when
we transcend the limits of phenomenality, or
when we look inward into the very reason of
things, all forms of separation and particulariza-
tion vanish, and taste becomes smell, sight
becomes hearing, etc., which is characteristic of
the supra-individual realm of ideality.

This being so, one who hears the world-sound
is no more nor less than he whose spiritual insight
has gone deep into the very foundation of existence, whose knowledge comprehends everything
and understands the reason of things, why they
are so and not otherwise, and whose life and
thought are in perfect harmony with the mind
that controls the destiny of the universe. He
has gone, as we say, to the other shore, he is a
Buddha, the enlightened.

If we wish to reach this stage of spirituality,
we must train ourselves not to be distracted by
the phenomenality of things, but directly to

envisage the ultimate essence of existence which is free from all modes of duality. In this, the perceiving and the perceived are not two, the hearing and the heard are not separate, the "I" and the "not I" are not what they appear to the senses. But there is but one reality and we can call it by any name. Buddhism is not particular in this matter of designation. You may call it God or reason or life or suchness or love, but let it only be noticed that you must not make it something altogether outside this universe, nor must you consider it a mere abstraction which has no business in this concrete world. To avoid this miscomprehension on the part of the untrained, Buddhism has called it "Sound" in this particular relation and declares that all things are of one Sound in which every discordant note is eternally synthesized. Not only the wind that blows, the waves that roar, the flute that whistles, but the mountains, rivers, oceans, suns, heavens, and everything that exists, are no more than so many variations of the Sound, eternal, ultimate, and unifying. Do not think that this is too hidden and esoteric; only train yourselves in the meditation of Buddhism, and you come to realize the truth of my statement. First, recognize the oneness of the ultimate principle, and think of its abiding in all things; and you will surely comprehend the point here somewhat mystically presented.

We often find another appellation attached to

Kwannon, the Goddess of Mercy, and that is Bodhisattva (*Bosatz* in Japanese and *Pu sa* in Chinese). It means a sentient being whose essence is wisdom, and is a title generally given to a highly enlightened, saintly Buddhist, or, in fact, to any sage of any faith.

What constitutes the essence of this being is love that sacrifices itself for the sake of others. A Bodhisattva will deny himself if he knows that by so doing he can save his fellow-beings from suffering, misery, ignorance, and self-delusion. Or he may assert himself if he sees that his creatures can be saved best through this assertion. His only object of life is to benefit others, his only principle of life is love, and his means of achieving this end and of realizing this principle is wisdom. He moves by love and regulates his movement by wisdom. His fountain of love is inexhaustible, and every feeling and thought and desire and resolution and everything else comes from this divine source; but his love does not move blindly, but most intelligently, for he is not only pure in heart but enlightened in mind. He knows that his self is a delusion, that if it exists at all it is in others and not in himself, that it embraces the whole universe and is not groaning within the narrowest and darkest cell of his own person.

Kwannon, therefore, is not only love incarnate, but a representation of wisdom and enlightenment. But as we have wisdom more emphatically represented by such Bodhisattvas as Monju (Mañjuçri in Sanskrit) and Seshi, we see in Kwannon the virtue of lovingkindness made most predominant, and for this reason the Bodhisattva has come to be represented as feminine. Whatever other virtues may be possessed by woman, she is adored for her tenderness, lovingkindness, longsuffering, and self-sacrifice. If she be without these qualities, however brilliantly intellectual or majestically imposing, she might be honored and respected, but she will never be an object of worship and adoration, for nobody will come before her, fall on his knees, and ask her for an all-embracing love—love which is pure, unselfish, and ennobling. Kwannon, therefore, will best be conceived as feminine.

When we ordinarily speak of love, we are apt to think of its blindness and exclusiveness. For love is contrasted with hate and associated with impulse. Because of the former, love necessarily discriminates and is prone to partiality and concentration; and because of the latter, love moves without regard to its consequence and knows not its ultimate purpose. But the love that makes up the being of Kwannon is not that kind of love, but that which is most comprehensive and universal as to embrace the entire universe, just and unjust, good and evil, pious and sacrilegious. In this love there is not a trace of partiality or discrimination. It is like rain that falls on all forms of vegetation, while each plant is benefited

in its own peculiar way.   It is, again, like the sun
that shines upon all forms of life, while the latter
make use of the sunshine each according to its
own nature.   The sun or rain thus benefiting
everything harbors no thought of discrimination.
Kwannon's love for all sentient beings is no more
than an exhibition of the universal energy of
animation and enlightenment, which creates,
fashions, and regulates the world.

It is now evident to you, I believe, that in
such spiritual love as that of Kwannon there is
no commercialism, no mercenary principle, which
says, "I give you so much and in return expect
from you such favor."   Kwannon abhors this
spirit of modern times which penetrates almost
every fibre of our civilization.   If you want to
worship Kwannon, she must be worshiped in
spirit and truth.   You must have your heart
cleansed of impurity, selfishness, and ignorance.
You must have your egoistic impulses baptized
by the water of enlightenment.   It is only when
you are pure in heart and humble in spirit that
you are ushered into the presence of Kwannon
Bosatz and become the recipient of all her infinite
blessings.   This is what Buddhism would call
grace.   Grace is not a special favor conferred
upon an unworthy subject, but the legitimate
result of self-purification.

Buddhists think love emanates from wisdom
or samâdhi or self-reflection.   As long as we are
sense-bound, we are not able to destroy the wall

of individuation and to realize the universal principle of love; and accordingly our love is limited, impulsive, and exclusive. In order to realize the love of Kwannon, we must shake off the filthy garment of selfishness by means of sound contemplation and earnest self-discipline. Unreflective persons live generally on the surface of things. They are unable to assort and systematize the ever-varying impressions which they get through the senses. They move according to blind impulses and selfish desires, by which they are bound hands and feet. They are unreasonable. They do not penetrate the bottom of things where lies the reason of existence. They may sometimes do some noble deeds, but that is not enlightenment, only madness. What is done by fits and starts does not constitute wisdom. The love that originates from an impure source cannot be made the foundation of our religious life.

When the love of Kwannon is made concrete, it expresses itself in various forms according to the needs of circumstance. In the *Pundarîka Sûtra* Kwannon is described as incarnating herself in many different personages. For instance, when she sees it most expedient to save a certain class of people through a certain mode of expression, she will assume the special mode and exercise all her influence in that capacity. She will be a philosopher, or merchant, or man of letters, or person of low birth, or anything else

as required by the occasion, while her sole aim
is to deliver all beings, without exception, from
ignorance and selfishness. Therefore, wherever
there is a heart groping in the dark, Kwannon
will not fail to extend her embracing arms.

It will be interesting in this connection to
compare the activity of Kwannon with what
Paul conceives of the activity of God as in his
first epistle to the Corinthians (xii, 4 *et seq.*):
"Now there are diversities of gifts, but the same
spirit. And there are differences of administra-
tions, but the same Lord. And there are diversities of operations, but it is the same God which
worketh all in all." . . . .

This conception of Kwannon, it seems to me,
has had a great influence in shaping the national
character of my countrymen. Whatever tenderness of heart they may have, they owe it to the
lovingkindness of Kwannon. Those who have
traveled in Japan must have seen a great many
shrines dedicated to her and multitudes of people
gathering before them and offering flowers and
incense and prayers. This may be a superstitious
practice,—this worshiping of a mythological
deity; but when we think what spiritual consolation and benefit the masses derive therefrom,
we must be a little lenient in our judgment of
their intellectual attainment. Being simple-
hearted, they believe in the response by Kwannon to their earnest prayers. The universal wave
of love is vibrating in every sentient being, and

when this innermost chord is touched through the deepest spiritual commotion one can suffer, it vibrates, and the vibration reaches the very source of life, which is the love of Kwannon, and there takes place the phenomenon called communion. The universal love-principle has thus made itself known to the human heart.

To add one more word. It seems to me that the Virgin Mary of your religion corresponds to the Buddhist Goddess of Mercy, Kwannon Bosatz. Human nature everywhere seems to request what Goethe calls "eternal femininity." Christians according to their needs have created Maria. Though she is a historical figure, she has been invested with all the necessary qualities that will satisfy their inner yearnings. Buddhists have Kwannon, who, whatever her historical standing in critical Buddhism, fully answers their religious cravings. From the Christian point of view, Kwannon is a Maria incarnate; and from the Buddhist standpoint, Maria is a representative of Kwannon among a class of people who designate themselves Christians. The truth must be one and humanity the same everywhere, and it is my earnest wish that the time will soon come when the East and the West will all join in the adoration of truth, disregarding all their accidental differences and contradictions.

BUDDHISM AND ORIENTAL CULTURE[1]

ONE of the features peculiar to Buddhism and which appeals most powerfully to Oriental imagination is that man's life is not limited to this existence only, that if he thinks, feels, and acts truthfully, nobly, virtuously, unselfishly, he will live forever in these thoughts, sentiments, and works; for anything good, beautiful, and true is in accordance with the reason of existence, and is destined to have a life eternal.

It is not the ideal of the Buddhist life to escape worldliness and to enter into eternal stillness, as is sometimes understood by Occidental scholars. Buddhists do not shun struggle and warfare. If a cause is worth contending for or defending, they will not hesitate to sacrifice for it not only this life but all of their future lives. They will appear upon this earth over and again and will not rest until they have gained the end, that is, until they have attained the ideal of life. Man, therefore, lives as long as his ideas and feelings conform to the reason of the universe. This is the Buddhist conception of life eternal.

[1]Address at the George Washington University, April, 1906.

If I am not mistaken, it was at the time of the Independence War, or it might have occurred somewhere in the Old Country,—you will pardon my imperfect memory,—but the fact is that a military officer who served as a spy for his native country was caught by the enemy and was sentenced to be hung. At the execution the officer exclaimed, "The pity is that I have only one life to sacrifice for my country." Pity indeed it was that the officer did not know the truth and fact that from his very corpse there have risen so many patriotic spirits breathing the same breath that he breathed. He was not dead, he was never hung, he did not vanish into an unknown region; but he is living a life eternal, he is being born generation after generation, not only in his own country, but also in my country, and in your country, and in fact all over the three thousand worlds (as they were believed to be existing in Hindu mythology).

In this respect a Buddhist general quite famous in the history of Japan had a decided advantage over the Christian officer just mentioned. The general is still worshiped in Japan as the type of loyalty and patriotism. He lived about six hundred years ago. Before the Emperor of the time came to know him, he was a rather obscure general and would have died without imprinting his immortal name on the pages of Japanese history. But Fate decreed otherwise, and he was requested by the Emperor to lead his royal

army against the invading enemy, who greatly
outnumbered his forces and was led by a very
able general. Masashigé, which is the name of
our hero, had his own plan as to how best to
make a stand against the onslaught of the over-
whelming enemy. But some ignorant court
favorite influenced the Emperor and the hero's
proposition could not prevail. He then knew
he was going to fight a losing battle, but determined to do his best under the circumstances,
if necessary to fight to the bitter end. At last
came the day, and the enemy developed the plan
as he had calculated. There was nothing for
him to do but to check the advance of the enemy
as long as he could, so that the Emperor could
find time enough to make his safe escape from
the capital. He fought most gallantly, and
repeatedly repulsed the furious attacks of the
enemy. But many times outnumbered, and
occupying a strategically disadvantageous position, and himself covered with many wounds,
he saw the uselessness of further resistance.
He then gathered his commanding generals
around him and asked them if they had anything
to desire in this life before they bid farewell to
all things earthly. They replied that they had
done everything within their power, their obli-
gations were completely filled, and there was
nothing more to be desired. But our hero,
Masashigé, made a solemn utterance: "I pray
that I be born seven times on this earth and

crush all the enemies of our Imperial House."
They all then drew their daggers and put an end
to their present lives.

I do not know how this story strikes you
Christian audience, but upon us Buddhists it
makes a very profound impression. It seems
to be pregnant with a great religious significance.
It is not altogether necessary to specify how
many times we are to be reborn. Let us only
have a thought or feeling that is worth preserving and actualizing, and we shall come to this
life as many times as is necessary to complete
the task, even to the end of the world. Let us
only do what is in accordance with the reason
of things, and the work, which is no more than the
world-reason actualized, will create a new agency
as needed through successive generations. This
corporeal existence, this particular temporary
combination of feelings and thoughts and desires,
may dissolve, may not last forever as it is, for
it is no more than an agent in the hands of the
world-soul to execute its own end. When it
decrees that its agent must put on a new garment,
this will take place as it is willed. "Let there
be light," it commands, and behold there it is!

It is not Buddhistic, therefore, to hanker after
personal immortality and to construct diversity
of theories to satisfy this illegitimate hankering.
Do whatever you think right and be sincere
with it and the work will take care of itself,
hankering or no hankering after immortality.

My Japanese hero gave an utterance to his inner feeling and conviction only to make his generals perfectly understand the significance of his and their work. He did not mean to come to this life exactly seven times, nor did he mean to continue his personal existence as he was individually. He did mean this, that his work should find its new executors in the form of a worshiper or an imitator or a successor or a disciple or a friend, who would be inspired by that noble example. And most certainly did he find a legion of his selves following closely behind his back. Are not all loyal and patriotic soldiers and sailors who died in the recent war with Russia all the incarnations of our most beloved hero-general, Masashigé? Did he not find his selves in all those brave, courageous, self-sacrificing hearts? Was he not leading in spirit all these soldiers to the execution of the work he once planned? Who says, then, that the hero breathed his last when he fought this losing battle some six hundred years ago? Is he not indeed still living in the heart of every patriotic and loyal citizen of Japan, nay, of any people that aspires to be a nation?

When the late commander Hirosé went to blockade the entrance to Port Arthur, he must have been inspired by the same sentiment which he expressed in his swan song; he must have become conscious of the immortality of the work in which he has thoroughly incarnated himself.

In his last utterance he put this in verse: "Though I may die here while executing this work, I will come back seven times over and again to discharge my duties for my country. I have nothing to fear, nothing to desire at the present moment. Calmly and smilingly I embark on this fated boat."[1] Can we not say here that the idea which was our long deceased hero himself, found its conscious expression in this brave Commander? Those who fell in the field and on the water were equally his incarnations, only with this difference that the former gave utterance to his conscious sentiment, while the latter remained mute, though in their inmost hearts the same sentiment was moving. If otherwise, how could they enjoy that serene contentedness which characterized every stricken warrior of my country in the recent war?

Some may say that this is fatalism or determinism, but every clear-headed thinker would see in this not a fatalistic conception of life but a hopeful solution of existence, a firm belief in the final triumph of good over evil, and the calm assurance that the individual lives as long as it identifies itself with a noble thought, worthy work, exalted sentiment, uplifting impulse, in short, with anything that cements the brotherly tie of all mankind. Those who are used to look at things from the individualistic point of view may not understand very clearly what I have so

[1] From memory.

far endeavored to explain to you; but the fact
is, however tenaciously we may cling to our individual existences, we are utterly helpless when
that which comprehends everything wills otherwise than our selfish desires; we have but to
submit meekly to the ordinance of the unknown power and to let it work out its own
destiny regardless of ourselves. When Schleier-
macher defines religion as a feeling of absolute
dependence, he has rightly laid his hand on that
indefinable, uncertain sense which lurks in the
dark recesses of every conscious mind,—the
sense which intuitively recognizes the weakness
of individuals as such, but which feels an immense
strength in their identification with a supra-
individual being or power. In this, it must be
evident to you, there is nothing fatalistic nor
fantastic.

All sincere Buddhists are firmly convinced of
the truth of non-egoism, and they do not think
that the value of an individual as such is ultimate. On account of this, they are not at all
disturbed at the moment of death; they calmly
accept the ordinance and let the world-destiny
accomplish what end it may have in view. This
freedom from the individualistic view of life
seems to have largely contributed to the perfection of the Japanese military culture known as
Bushido. Old Japanese soldiers, nobles, and men
of letters, therefore, displayed a certain sense of
playfulness even at the most critical moment

whon the question of life and death was to be
decided without the least hesitation. This playfulness, as I view it, stands in a marked contrast
to the pious, prayerful attitude of the Christians
in their dying moments.

Ota Dôkwan, a great Japanese statesman-
general of some four hundred years ago, was
assassinated in his own castle by a band of spies
sent by his enemy. They surrounded him when
he was altogether unarmed. He was stabbed,
'and he fell on the ground, covered with wounds
and helpless. One of the assassins approached
closer, and applying the dagger at the victim's
throat to finish their cowardly work, he asked
what the unfortunate general had to say before
he bade farewell to this world. The general
most calmly answered:

> "At the moment like this
> It must be a struggle indeed
> To part with this life so dear,
> If I had not abandoned altogether
> The thought of ego, which is a non-reality."

Finding peace of heart in this solution of life,
Buddhists, whatever their social positions, are
ever ready to sacrifice their lives for a cause
which demands them. They know that the
present individual existences will come to an
end, they will not be able to see the faces dearest
to them, to hear the voices tenderest to them,
as they depart from this world; but they know
at the same time that spiritually they live for-

ever and are in constant communication with
their friends, that they never lead a solitary,
unconnected life in some invisible region.   What
Buddhism has contributed to Japanese culture
is its higher conception of life and nobler interpretation of death.

Buddhists do not think that "I" is "I" and
"you" is "you" when each of us is separated
from the other.   "I" is possible when "you"
exists, so with "you" who is possible through
the existence of "I."   This consideration is very
important, as it constitutes one of the fundamental principles of Buddhist ethics.   For according to Buddhism an unconditional assertion of
egoism is due to the ignorance of the significance
of the individual.   Most people imagine that the
individual is a final reality, stands by itself, has
nothing to do with other fellow-individuals; in
fact their existence is tolerated only so far as it
does not interfere with his own interests.   They
first build a formidable fort around individualism
and look down at their surroundings, thinking
that the position must be defended at all costs.
For it is their conception of life that with the
downfall of individualism the universe goes to
pieces.

The Oriental mode of thinking, however, differs
from this.   We take our standpoint first on that
which transcends individuals, or we take into
our consideration first that which comprehends
all finite things, that which determines the

destiny of the universe; and then we come down into this world of relativity and conditionality, and believe that the earth will sooner or later pass away according to the will of that which controls it.   That is to say, individuals will not stay here forever, though the whole which comprises individuals will.   Therefore, Oriental ethics considers it of paramount importance to preserve the whole at all hazards, whatever may be the fate of individuals.

For instance, suppose my country is threatened by a powerful enemy, and I will, when called for, sacrifice everything personal and try to do my best for the conservation of my national honor and safety.   This is what is called patriotism. My parents are old and they are not able to take care of themselves, and I will do everything for their comfort and alleviate the loneliness of their declining age.   Did they not bring me up to this stage of manhood?   Did they not go through all forms of hardship for my sake?   Did they not care for me with infinite tenderness of heart? Do I not owe them all that I am to-day?   Did they not help me to this position and enable me to do whatever is within my power for the welfare and preservation of the whole to which I belong?   When I think of this, the feeling of gratitude weighs heavily on me, and I endeavor to be relieved of it by doing all acts of loving-kindness to my parents.   This is what you call filial piety, and the same consideration will apply to the cases of teachers, elder people, friends, and family.

Whatever be the defects of Oriental ethics,—and I think they are not a few,—I firmly believe that what makes Oriental culture so unique is due to the emphasis laid upon patriotism, filial piety, faithfulness, and abnegation of self.

*   *   *

Before concluding, I wish to add a few words as a Buddhist subject of Japan. All the world knows what Japan has achieved so far in the history of mankind, especially what she has accomplished in her gigantic struggle with a most powerful nation of Europe. There must have been many causes and conditions through a happy combination of which Japan was able to do what she has done; and among those conditions I would count the influence of American friendship and sympathy as one of the most powerful. If America had tried to play some high-handed diplomacy, imitating some of the European powers, she could have easily seized my country and held it under subjection since Commodore Perry's entrance into Uraga. The fact that the United States did not stoop to play a mean trick upon Japan helped not a little to lift her to the present position. For that reason, we, people of Japan, owe a great deal to you, people of the United States of America.

As a Buddhist I have been long thinking how best to repay this special favor received from the friendly people among whom I am traveling now. You have everything you need in the line of material, industrial, commercial civilization. By this I do not mean that you are wanting in spiritual culture and moral refinement, but I am inclined to think that it would not be altogether inappropriate to ask you to get more and more acquainted with what constitutes Oriental culture and religious belief. And it shall be my duty and pleasure to make such an opportunity of mutual understanding readily possible in every way. Accordingly, I thank you, ladies and gentlemen, for your efforts which have resulted in this enjoyable meeting with each other.

THE STORY OF DEER PARK[1]

BRAHMADATTA, king of Bârânasî, one day
went out hunting in the forest, where he
saw two groups of deer, each of which consisted
of five hundred individuals and was escorted by
a leader. One of them wore a coat decorated
in the colors of the seven precious jewels. He
was one of the former incarnations of Bodhisattva
Shâkyamuni, while the other leader was that
of Devadatta.

The Deer-Bodhisattva was greatly grieved at
the sight of so many of his fellow-animals being
killed by the royal hunting party. His great
loving heart was stirred to its core and he could
not endure any longer to witness the butchery.
He determined to see the king in person and to
have the matter settled in a more humane way.
When he moved forward, a veritable shower of
arrows greeted him, but he was not to be overcome and made a steady advance towards the
king. Observing this indomitable resolution displayed by the Deer-Bodhisattva, the king ordered

[1]Deer Park in Benares was the place where Buddha
first caused the Wheel of the Good Law to revolve. See the
beginning of the *Sutra of Forty-two Chapters*.

the party to cease shooting and allowed him to approach unmolested.

Said the deer, "It grieves my heart to see so many innocent creatures sacrificed merely to gratify your selfish passions. If you wish to have us for your table, we could arrange to send you each day one victim, to be chosen alternately from our two groups. Only let us be spared from a general massacre." The king consented to this arrangement.

For a while the plan worked without obstruction, but now it happened that a prospective mother-doe had to be chosen for the victim. She was exceedingly mortified over the ill fate, not for her own sake, but for that of her baby that was coming to see the light ere long. She went to Devadatta, to whose group she belonged, and asked him for a special dispensation, saying that "It being my fate to be sacrificed this time, I have no complaint to make as far as I alone am concerned, but the baby I am about to give birth to is not to be deprived of existence with its mother, for its doomsday has not yet arrived. Would that your majesty would contrive some means to execute the plan as arranged and yet to save my innocent child."

But Devadatta was cold-hearted and bluntly said, "Who in the world desires to be killed? Does not every living creature wish to preserve its life as long as it can? The turn is yours. Be gone, and no more of this wailing."

The doe thought within herself that she did not at all deserve the wrath of Devadatta, and this added to her grief and despondence. But a happy idea occurred to her. As the last resort she resolved to go and see the Bodhisattva, asking him if he knew some way of saving her at this critical moment. Being questioned by him as to the steps taken by Devadatta concerning this matter, she said: "My king has no compassion for me, but is enraged without due cause—it seems to me. I know, however, that your love is boundless and that you are the last refuge for the helpless and despondent. This is the reason why I, though not belonging to your group, am here to ask for your infinite wisdom."

The Bodhisattva took a great pity on the despairing mother-doe and thought: "If she has to be sacrificed, her innocent unborn child will have to share the same fate. If a substitute were to be selected, an injustice would be done. The only person that could take her place without disturbing the prearranged order is nobody else than myself. I shall then be the victim this time instead of the mother-doe."

Coming to this conclusion, the Bodhisattva offered himself to the king as the victim of the day. Asked the king, "What brings you here? Are all your deer gone already?" Replied the Bodhisattva, "Your grace and benevolence is known the world over, and nobody would dare violate your injunctions; but it grieves me to see the propagation of my race unnecessarily checked. I have come to the knowledge of such a case to-day and I pity it. If I make any change in the order of victims as arranged at the outset, it will be unreasonable. If I do not save the mother, it is against the nature of a sentient being. This is the reason why I present myself to-day before you. Life is short and everything is subject to the law of impermanence. Why shall I not practise lovingkindness while I am yet alive?"

The king was greatly moved by the words of the Bodhisattva and expressed his deep appreciation as follows: "It is myself and not you that belongs to the beastly creation. I am a deer in a man's form. Though you are in appearance a lower animal, you are in heart a human being. What makes one differ from another is not outward signs but inner reason. If endowed with a loving heart, though a beast in form, one is human. From this day I swear not to delight any more in partaking of animal flesh. Fear not, my friend, but be at ease forever."

It was in this wise that the forest was reserved for the deer to roam about in as they pleased and came to be known as Deer Park.

THE STORY OF THE GEM-HUNTING[1]

IN ancient times there was a king who had among his valuable possessions a precious stone which he most highly prized. An attendant of his one day dropped it accidentally in a very deep lake which was in his palace garden. The king was greatly troubled and immediately made an inquiry among his subjects whether there was any one who could locate the precious treasure in the water and safely restore it to his hands, adding that such a one would receive a handsome reward.

There was among his retainers a man called Clear-Sighted, whose optical power was considered almost supernatural, and everybody thought that he was the man who could find the lost gem in the lake, however deep and wide it might be. The man was brought before the king and was directly commissioned to make a search for the gem.

Clear-Sighted dived deep into the water and tried to locate the precious stone at its bottom. But, singularly, his sight did not avail him to any

---

[1]This story was told by the Rev. Shaku to illustrate Chapter 9 of the *Sutra of Forty-two Chapters.*

great extent, for he was utterly unable to observe it anywhere. The harder he strove the dimmer became his sight. Completely disappointed at this unexpected discovery of his shortsightedness, he came out from the bottom of the lake, and reported his miserable failure to the king, whose mortification now knew no bounds.

The king did not know what to do; he could not reconcile himself to the new situation. A long consultation was held again, but no one seemed to be able to solve the problem in a practical way. In despair they finally came to test a most unusual method, which seemed almost absurd and ridiculous.

They knew there was a man called Sightless, and thought if Clear-Sighted was of no avail this blind man might be found useful in such a case as this, which was so extraordinary. At any rate, the attempt would not result in making the situation worse. Things miraculous have frequently been performed by the blind, and why not in this case?

Sightless was sent for and asked to go down into the water and find the lost gem. The man went down as he was told, without any pro-testation. When he came out after a short time, the treasure was in his hand. The king was overjoyed and rewarded him most gen-erously

The moral of this allegorical story is that much cunning and great learning are not the most effective means, as ordinarily supposed, to obtain the priceless gem of religious truth, but that the simple in heart and poor in spirit will find the way to heavenly bliss.

THE SACRIFICE FOR A STANZA[1]

IN one of his many previous births on this
earth, Buddha appeared as a son of a Hindu
prince. Desirous to gain spiritual insight into
the ultimate reason of existence, he retired to
the solitude and quietness of the mountains, as
was customary in India, and became deeply
absorbed in meditation. He thought: "Life is
misery; it is nothing but a series of sufferings.
How can I escape this everlasting torture?
Unless I gain all-knowledge and grasp eternal
life and realize perfect bliss, it is of no use to
come here and live this life repeatedly. Of what
worth is this life to me, to all beings, unless we
escape the curse of ignorance by penetrating the
ultimate foundation of existence? Until I gain
enlightenment and immortality, I will not move
from my seat which I have taken here under this
tree, and I will bring all my spiritual powers
into activity toward that end. If I am fortunate
enough to realize it, I will not keep the spiritual

---

[1]From the *Mahânirvâna Sutra* (Nanjo's Catalogue,
No. 113). This story was told to explain the miraculous
origin of the famous stanza beginning with "Anicca vata
sankhâra." See the sermon "The Phenomenal and the
Supra-phenomenal." (See p. 111.)

bliss all to myself, but will proclaim it to all
sentient beings on earth, and enlighten them,
and make them happy as well."

It was midnight and silence reigned upon the
earth. Buddha was deeply enwrapt in his
thoughts. Suddenly he heard a voice which
came from nowhere he knew. It did not sound
like a human voice; it was clear, penetrating,
and resounding; he thought the universe was
filled with a resonant reverberation of this
mysterious voice. As he listened to it he could
understand these two lines of a gâthâ:

> "All component things are transient;
> The law is to be born and die."

When he could make out these two lines, a
spiritual illumination came over his mind, and
he felt in himself something superhuman, something divine. His mind became so widened as
to embrace the entire universe, and he experienced a feeling of inexpressible joy. He looked
across the valley, and lo! there his gaze fell on a
hideous monster straightway confronting him.
Buddha was bewildered and did not know what
this all meant.

The monster was a Yaksha, so inhuman and
awe-inspiring, with the eye so furiously glaring
on Buddha, and the mouth stained with dripping
blood. It was this monstrous devil that had just
recited those two lines which had so greatly
inspired him that he thought they came from a
mouth other than that of this evil genius.

This unexpected and altogether mysterious appearance, however, did not at all disconcert Buddha, as he was still under the spiritual spell induced by those two noble lines. His only thought which he had at that moment was that the lines were not quite complete and that something was needed to make them so. Stating only the fact of universal impermanence, they did not show the way to escape it or to transcend it. The reason why we mortals are groaning under the yoke of karmaic causation is that we are yet ignorant of its true significance, that we have not yet severed the tie of birth and death.

So said Buddha to the Yaksha: "Those lines which you have just recited are beautiful but incomplete. Let me have the remaining two, which will complete the gâthâ. For this is not only for my own benefit, but for the benefit of all mankind. Pray be good enough to disclose what is yet kept behind."

Said the monster: "I will gladly comply with your request, but at this very moment I suffer from a bodily need and have not strength enough to recite the remaining two lines for you. My empty stomach must be fed and I live on human flesh. Would you first satisfy my appetite? I should then be able to let you have what you desire."

Buddha said: "I am ready at any moment to sacrifice myself, O Yaksha, but when I exist no more, who in this world will transmit these

lines all complete to posterity? The truth will
then be eternally lost to mankind. I, therefore,
beseech you to recite those two remaining lines
before I die, and I will engrave the whole stanza
on this rock standing near by. After this is
done, you can dispose of my body as you please.
The stanza thus left on the stone will be noticed
some day by a passer-by and brought out to the
world for the enlightenment of my fellow-beings."

The Yaksha said: "As you are so earnest and
sincere, I grant your wish. Listen to my reci-
tation:

> "Transcending birth and death,
> How blissful is the Absolute!"

When the Yaksha finished, Buddha made one
of his fingers bleed, and with the dripping blood
inscribed the whole stanza on the rock. This
being done, Buddha threw himself over the
precipice in order to fulfill his promise. But
behold! at this crisis the hideous vampire suddenly changed his features, he became Sakrendra,
a reigning god of the heavens and a most powerful guardian angel of Buddhism. Buddha,
falling into the abyss, was miraculously received
in the arms of this god, who now honored and
revered him. The heavens showered flowers and
the universe resounded with divine music.

BUDDHIST VIEW OF WAR[1]

"THIS triple world[2] is my own possession. All the things therein are my own children. Sentient or non-sentient, animate or inanimate, organic or inorganic, the ten thousand things in this world are no more than the reflections of my own self. They come from the one source. They partake of the one body. Therefore I cannot rest quiet, until every being, even the smallest possible fragment of existence, is settled down in its proper appointment. I do not mind what long eons it will take to finish this gigantic work of salvation. I work at the end of eternity when all beings are peacefully and happily nestled in an infinite loving heart."

This is the position taken by the Buddha, and we, his humble followers, are but to walk in his wake.

Why, then, do we fight at all?

Because we do not find this world as it ought to be. Because there are here so many perverted

---

[1]Reproduced from THE OPEN COURT, May, 1904.

[2]The "triple world" (*triloka*) is a common Buddhist term for "universe." The three worlds are "the world of desire" (*kâmaloka*), "the world of bodily form" (*rûpaloka*), and "the immaterial world" (*arûpaloka*).

creatures, so many wayward thoughts, so many
ill-directed hearts, due to ignorant subjectivity.
For this reason Buddhists are never tired of combating all productions of ignorance, and their
fight must be to the bitter end.   They will show
no quarter.   They will mercilessly destroy the
very root from which arises the misery of this life.
To accomplish this end, they will never be afraid
of sacrificing their lives, nor will they tremble
before an eternal cycle of transmigration.   Corporeal existences come and go, material appear-
ances wear out and are renewed.   Again and
again they take up the battle at the point where
it was left off.

But all the Buddhas and Bodhisattvas never
show any ill-will or hatred toward enemies.
Enemies—the enemies of all that is good—are
indeed wicked, avaricious, shameless, hell-born,
and, above all, ignorant.   But are they not,
too, my own children for all their sins?   They
are to be pitied and enlightened, not persecuted.
Therefore, what is shed by Buddhists is not
blood,—which, unfortunately, has stained so
many pages in the history of religion,—but tears
issuing directly from the fountain-head of lovingkindness.

The most powerful weapon ever used by Buddha
in the subjugation of his wayward children is
the practice of non-atman (non-egotism).   He
wielded it more effectively than any deadly,
life-destroying weapons.   When he was under the

Bodhi-tree absorbed in meditation on the non-atmanness of things, fiends numbering thousands tried in every way to shake him from his transcendental serenity; but all to no purpose. On the contrary, the arrows turned to heavenly flowers, the roaring clamor to a paradisiacal music, and even the army of demons to a host of celestials. And do you wonder at it? Not at all! For what on earth can withstand an absolutely self-freed heart overflowing with loving-kindness and infinite bliss?

And this example should be made the ideal of every faithful Buddhist. Whatever calling he may have chosen in this life, let him be freed from ego-centric thoughts and feelings. Even when going to war for his country's sake, let him not bear any hatred towards his enemies. In all his dealings with them let him practise the truth of non-atman. He may have to deprive his antagonist of the corporeal presence, but let him not think there are atmans, conquering each other. From a Buddhist point of view, the significance of life is not limited to the present incarnation. We must not exaggerate the significance of individuals, for they are not independent and unconditional existences. They acquire their importance and a paramount meaning, moral and religious, as soon as their fate becomes connected with the all-pervading love of the Buddha, because then they are no more particular individuals filled with egotistic thoughts

and impulses, but have become love incarnate.
They are so many representative types of one
universal self-freed love. If they ever have to
combat one another for the sake of their home
and country,—which under circumstances may
become unavoidable in this world of particularity,—let them forget their egotistic passions,
which are the product of the atman conception—
of selfishness. Let them, on the contrary, be filled
with the lovingkindness of the Buddha; let them
elevate themselves above the horizon of the
mine and thine. The hand that is raised to strike
and the eye that is fixed to take aim, do not
belong to the individual, but are the instruments
utilized by a principle higher than transient
existence. Therefore, when fighting, fight with
might and main, fight with your whole heart,
forget your own self in the fight, and be free
from all atman thought.

It is most characteristic of our religion, as we
understand it, that while Buddha emphasized
the paramount significance of synthetic love, he
never lost sight of the indispensableness of analyt-
ical intellect. He extended his sympathy to all
creatures as his own children and made no discrimination in his boundless compassion. But
at the same time he was not ignorant of the fact
that there were good as well as bad people, that
there were innocent hearts as well as guilty ones.
Not that some were more favored by the Buddha
than others, but they were enabled to acquire

more of the love of the Buddha. One rain falls on all kinds of plants; but they do not assimilate the water in the same fashion. Buddha's love is universal, but our hearts, being fashioned of divergent karmas, receive it in different ways. He knows where they are finally led to, for his love is unintermittently working out their salvation, though they themselves be utterly unconscious of it.

Above all things, there is the truth, and there are many roads leading to it. It may seem at times that they collide and oppose one another. But let us rest confident that finally every ill will come to some good.

AT THE BATTLE OF NAN-SHAN HILL[1]

ALL that I can say is, "It beggars descrip-
tion!" Verily, it is the acme of brutality
and recklessness conceived in this world of individualization (*nâmarûpa*). Even the fight between
the Asura and Sakrendra, the demons and the
angels, witnessed by our Buddha, seems here to
sink into insignificance.

As far as my unaided eye can see, nature
around me is calm. The Tai-lien Bay to the
left and the Kin-chou Bay to the right, both as
tranquil as mirrors, and above us and over the
Nan-Shan Hill, where directly in our front the
Russian fortifications stand, the sky expands in
majestic serenity. Nothing suggests the awful
carnage which there is enacted. Guns roar,
bombs burst, but we do not see whence they
come, and their knell only offsets the solemnity
of these peaceful surroundings. But when I look
through a powerful field-glass, I behold the hill-
sides strewn with dead and wounded, and soldiers
rush onward over these wretches, while the

---

[1]Reproduced from THE OPEN COURT, December, 1904.

enemies on the hill are madly scrambling, stumbling, and falling.   I shudder at the sight.

*   *   *

Still more appalling is a visit to the battle-field after the fight.   Yesterday, when I viewed Nan-Shan Hill from a distance, imagination lent enchantment to the spectacle, and at times the cannonade even impressed me with grandeur. But I am now confronting actualities,—actualities whose terror and horror can never be forgotten. From the top of yonder hill, where, under the calm summer sky, nature smiled in beauty, I could form no true conception of the tragedy, which, as I see now, took place here in unparalleled fury and madness.   What a strange paradox is this contrast,—a most horrible catastrophe of human life happening in the most delightful surroundings!   It makes me meditate again on the doctrine of our teacher.

*   *   *

Buddhism provides us with two entrances through which we can reach the citadel of perfect truth.   One is the gate of love (*karunâ*) and the other the gate of knowledge (*prajnâ*).   The former leads us to the world of particulars and the latter to the realm of the absolute.   By knowledge we aspire to reach the summit of spiritual enlightenment; by love we strive to rescue our fellow-creatures from misery and crime.   View the vicissitudes of things from the unity and eternity of the religious standpoint, the Dharmadhatu, and everything is one, is on the same plane, and I learn to neglect the worldly distinction made between friend and foe, tragedy and comedy, war and peace, samsâra and nirvâna, passion (*kleça*) and enlightenment (*bodhi*). A philosophical calm pervades my soul and I feel the contentment of Nirvâna. For there is nothing, as far as I can see, that does not reflect the glory of Buddha. Even in the midst of this transcendent universality, however, my heart aches with a pain, undefinable yet insuppressible. Love for all sentient beings asserts itself, and that frigid indifference of the intellect gives way.

And why was it necessary that the many horrors of this present war should come to pass? Why had those poor soldiers to sacrifice their lives? In every one of them a warm heart has been beating, and now they are all lying on the ground in piles, stiff and stark like logs.

O Mother Earth! All these my fellow-creatures, it is true, are made of the same stuff of which thou art made. But do not their lives partake of something not of the earth earthy, altogether unlike thyself, ånd, indeed, more than mere gross matter? Are theirs not precious human souls which can be engaged in the works of peace and enlightenment? Why art thou so gravely dumb, when thou art covered with things priceless that are being dissolved into their primitive elements?

In this world of particulars, the noblest **and**

greatest thing one can achieve is to combat evil
and bring it into complete subjection.   The moral
principle which guided the Buddha throughout
his twelve years of preparation and in his forty-
eight years of religious wanderings, and which
pervades his whole doctrine, however varied it
may be when practically applied, is nothing else
than the subjugation of evil.   To destroy the
ninety-eight major and eighty-four thousand
minor evils, that are constantly tormenting
human souls on this earth, was the guiding thought
of the Buddha.   Therefore, every follower of the
Buddha builds a great boat of love, launches it
on the great ocean of birth and death, steers it
with the great rudder of faith, and sails forth
with a steadfast mind through the whirling tempest of egotistic desires and passions.   No Buddhist will ever relax his energy, until every one
of his fellow-creatures be safely carried over to
the other shore of perfect bliss.

War is an evil and a great one, indeed.   But
war against evils must be unflinchingly prose-
cuted till we attain the final aim.   In the present
hostilities, into which Japan has entered with great
reluctance, she pursues no egotistic purpose, but
seeks the subjugation of evils hostile to civilization, peace, and enlightenment.   She deliber-
ated long before she took up arms, as she was
well aware of the magnitude and gravity of the
undertaking.   But the firm conviction of the
justice of her cause has endowed her with an

indomitable courage, and she is determined to carry the struggle to the bitter end.

Here is the price we must pay for our ideals— a price paid in streams of blood and by the sacrifice of many thousands of living bodies. However determined may be our resolution to crush evils, our hearts tremble at the sight of this appalling scene.

Alas! How much dearer is the price still going to be? What enormous losses are we going to suffer through the evil thoughts of our enemy, not to speak of the many injuries which our poor enemy himself will have to endure? All these miserable soldiers, individually harmless and innocent of the present war, are doomed to a death not only unnatural, but even inhuman!

Indeed, were it not for the doctrine of love taught by the Buddha, which should elevate every individual creature to the realm of a pure spirituality, we would, in the face of the terrible calamities that now befall us, be left to utter destruction and without any consolation whatever. Were it not for the belief that the bloom of truly spiritual light will, out of these mutilated, disfigured, and decomposing corpses, return with renewed splendor, we would not be able to stand these heart-rending tribulations even for a moment. Were it not for the consolation that these sacrifices are not brought for an egotistic purpose, but are an inevitable step toward the final realization of enlightenment, how could I, poor mortal, bear these experiences of a hell let loose on earth?

The body is but a vessel for something greater than itself.   Individuality is but a husk containing something more permanent.   Let us, then, though not without losing tenderness of heart, bravely confront our ordeal.

*   *   *

I came here with a double purpose.   I wished to have my faith tested by going through the greatest horrors of life, but I also wished to inspire, if I could, our valiant soldiers with the ennobling thoughts of the Buddha, so as to enable them to die on the battlefield with the confidence that the task in which they are engaged is great and noble.   I wished to convince them of the truths that this war is not a mere slaughter of their fellow-beings, but that they are combating an evil, and that, at the same time, corporeal annihilation really means a rebirth of soul, not in heaven, indeed, but here among ourselves.   I believe I did my best to impress these ideas upon the soldiers' hearts; and my own sentiments I express in the following stanza, one of the many poems composed on the field of battle:

> Here, marching on Nan-Shan,
>   Storming its topmost crest,
> Have thousands of brave men
>   With dragon valor pressed.
> Before the foe my heart
>   Is calmed, composure-blessed,
> While belching cannons sing
>   A lullaby of rest.

AN ADDRESS DELIVERED AT A SERVICE HELD IN MEMORY OF THOSE WHO DIED IN THE RUSSO-JAPANESE WAR

(At the Golden Gate Hall, November, 1905.)

I AM requested here to-night to speak concerning our brethren who fell in the greatest
and most sanguinary war of modern times,—the
war that only recently was brought to a conclusion. But what shall I say? Shall I eulogize
the glory of their death? or shall I depict to
you the unimaginable horrors of war? or have
I to praise the prowess and success of our Japanese army and navy? or have I to dwell upon
the innumerable sufferings of our people at
home which have been brought about by the
war? I am not, however, an orator in any sense
of the word, and am utterly disqualified for the
task laid down before me, either to glorify the
dead or to denounce war. All that I can do is
to look upon the matter from a purely religious
viewpoint and to express my own ideas concerning those unfortunate dead who fell in the defense
of our fatherland. And, if I can, let me try to
make their departed spirits calmly repose where
they fell, while I demonstrate to those left behind

204

the fact that the immortality of the soul consists in the realization of noble deeds, and not in the continuation of personality after death, if such a thing be at all possible

* * *

When we are talking in the abstract we are apt to see only the bright side of war—its inevitableness, its sublimity, its awe-inspiring scene, its perfect organization, its earnestness, its patriotism, and so forth, and we forget at what price these glorious things are bought, we forget that war is the most horrible evil of human life, that killing one another with whatever beautiful excuse is a proof of moral depravity, that our mission here under the sun is not to destroy life, but to preserve and develop it. Are we not here to realize the ideals of universal brotherhood and eternal peace? Are we not here to help one another and to promote our mutual welfare? Are we not here to make a grand universal home in which everybody is respected, believed, and loved? Let me ask, then: Does war in any way subserve this end? does it augment our happiness? does it make us respect one another? does it bring more life into the world? Let those who would answer affirmatively these questions go to one of those bloody battlefields in Manchuria and tell us what is disclosed before their unprejudiced eyes.

This is one of the most hotly contested hills around Port Arthur. Battles have been fought all morning and all afternoon, positions have been alternately taken by our soldiers and enemies. Battalions after battalions have been rushed forward only to fall under the veritable showers of death-dealing missiles, while those fortunate ones who have escaped the hell of fire are greeted with a phalanx of cold steel. And what do we see before us now? Hundreds of hundreds of dead and wounded are scattered all over the hill, friends and foes indiscriminately. Are not some of them yet writhing in their last agony? Where does that faint groaning come? Were not those stark corpses the most lively, most briskly moving bodies a few hours ago? Were not a courageous heart and a noble mind abiding in each one of them? The moon is just rising, and her pale light but enhances the ghastliness of the sight. The perfect stillness of horror! And I speak of this from my personal experience.

Now let me again ask: From where do these soldiers come? They must have parents—some of whom are aged and perhaps decrepit—sisters and brothers, and some of them must be even husbands and fathers on whom tender women and helpless children are depending. Now that their mainstays are gone and their beloved are forever departed, grief and suffering indescribable must be reigning in all these thousands of homes. Some of them, reduced to abject poverty and utter helplessness, must go begging or to self-destruction to save themselves from shame. What wrong did they commit to be thus terribly punished? The wrong, if it be so called, was that they had able-bodied, strong-minded sons or husbands. What a heart-rending ordeal they have to pass!

This most saddening fact is brought home more forcibly when we are personally related to the unfortunate dead.

News of victory is welcome and we feel elated over it. But think of the price we have paid for it with thousands of precious human lives. And especially when we find some of our personal friends and acquaintances mentioned among the dead or seriously wounded, how depressingly the news weighs upon us! I often spend many hours at a time brooding over the sad event, my thoughts being deeply buried in the unfathomable problems of philosophy and religion, which have baffled many a wise man ever since the dawn of intellect. Though I have formed in my humble way my own *welt-* and *lebensanschauung* with which I interpret the affairs of the world and the phenomena of soul-life, I cannot help being struck with the calamities which follow in the wake of war. I am not necessarily absorbed in pessimism, but I feel an unspeakable feeling at the bottom of my heart and with wonder and awe think of a power by whose hand the course of this life and the destiny of the universe are directed.

Why is human life so cheap? Why can it not be made to resist flying lead? Why is it so frail as to succumb to the thrust of cold steel? Why was it not made invulnerable, so that water could not drown and fire could not consume? Man, how conceited thou art when thy pulse beats and thy blood is warm! How haughty, god-like, immortal thou art when thou sittest alone and uninterruptedly pursuest thy egotistic schemes and intrigues! But, alas! thy dreams depart and thou must face cold, brutal realities. What a pitiful sight thou presentest now! Thou runnest against a mass of granite, cement, and steel, or against the exploding nitroglycerin, which is thine own handiwork, and thou art reduced to atoms, thou art blown to nothingness, whence thou perhaps didst come. How fragile thou art! Is this not the thought that agitates those who reflect upon the horrors of war and the destiny of mankind?

But are we not made for some other and better purposes than being merely material, physical, sensual, earthly, corporeal? Has not human existence more significance than a mere sentient organism whose life is as delicate as a drop of dew? Are we not capable of being more than what we appear to the senses? Are we not also living in a realm which transcends the world of sense and perception? To these questions I answer most definitely, and say "yes." However weak and helpless and flickering like a solitary lamplight before the wind, we are most assuredly more than a corporeal existence. Our limbs may be torn to pieces, our brains be smashed to nothing, our bones be ground to powder; but our deeds, our thoughts, our feelings will survive. It is in the realm of sense and perception that we are born and die. In the realm where our true being resides there is no such thing as birth and death. In the spiritual kingdom ours is an eternal growth, a perpetual unfolding, a never-ending development. The flesh will decay and return to dust, but the spirit which consists of our noble deeds and thoughts forever rejuvenates itself. It is like the snake's shedding its skin: the bodily existence is the skin, which is cast off whenever the spirit so desires. It is immaterial how the body fares, for the spirit is the master and its commands have to be obeyed at all hazards. The spirit decides when and how its outer integument shall be renewed. To be more exact and literal, the spirit which is immortal has limited itself to effect its own differentiation and development under the bodily condition. The body is therefore needed to complete the mission of the spirit, but the body is so created as to be subservient to the spirit and to be willing to carry out what the latter wills.

In ancient Oriental mythology we have a divine phenix, the only one of its kind and of remarkable beauty, that living five or six hun-

dred years in the Arabian desert built a funeral
pile of spices and aromatic gums, ignited it with
the fanning of its wings, sang a melodious dirge,
and burned itself in the all-purifying fire, only to
come out again in the freshness of youth and to
continue its former life. Is it not a wonderful
bird, this divine phenix of eternal life? But
more wonderful indeed is our spiritual life.

I believe all Japanese are familiar with the
story of Kusunoki Masashigé, who exclaimed in
his last moment that he would be reborn seven
times and protect his royal family against the
enemy. You also know well the anecdote of the
late Commander Hirosé, who expressed the same
sentiment in one of his last poems. But in point
of fact these heroes are not only seven times
reborn, but infinitely, so long as this universe
endureth and humanity survives. Do not think
for a moment that this is merely theoretical and
has no concrete significance. Far from it. We
who are breathing to-day the spirit of the illus-
trious general and the valiant sailor are no
more nor less than their reincarnations. Those
who come after us and become possessed of the
same sentiment are their and our spiritual descendants. Rebirth does not mean the reawakening of
the dead. Reincarnation does not mean the
resuscitation of a dried-up mummy. The immortality of the soul does not mean the continuation
of the individual soul as conceived by most
religionists. The spirit is not a thing material

and sensual, however ethereally or astrally you may conceive it. It is a transcendental existence, which knows no limiting conditions such as space, time, or causation. Where you feel a noble feeling, where you think a beautiful thought, where you do a self-sacrificing deed, there is the spirit making itself felt in your consciousness.

There is but one great spirit and we individuals are its temporal manifestations. We are eternal when we do the will of the great spirit; we are doomed when we protest against it in our egotism and ignorance. We obey, and we live. We defy, and we are thrown into the fire that quencheth not. Our bodily existences are like the sheaths of the bamboo sprout. For the growth of the plant it is necessary to cast one sheath after another. It is not that the body-sheath is negligible, but that the spirit-plant is more essential and its wholesome growth of paramount importance. Let us, therefore, not absolutely cling to the bodily existence, but, when necessary, sacrifice it for a better thing. For this is the way in which the spirituality of our being asserts itself.

This being the case, war is not necessarily horrible, provided that it is fought for a just and honorable cause, that it is fought for the maintenance and realization of noble ideals, that it is fought for the upholding of humanity and civilization. Many material human bodies may be destroyed, many humane hearts be broken, but from a broader point of view these sacrifices are so many phenixes consumed in the sacred fire of spirituality, which will arise from the smouldering ashes reanimated, ennobled, and glorified. The spirit which dwelt in them and brought them to the altar now assumes another material expression in the form of coming generations. Those fallen in the field are returning to dust in order to nourish vegetation, or, as the Japanese would express it, to fill the hungry stomach of the wild dog. But this is true only of their particular bodily forms. As to the spirit, it has not gone up to a mythical region which some religious people call heaven. It has not vanished into the air in the fashion of a ghost. Nor is it sitting by the so-called Heavenly Father encircled by a host of angels. We Buddhists are not believers in fiction, superstition, or mythology. We are followers of truth and fact. And what we actually see around us is that the departed spirits are abiding right among ourselves, for we have the most convincing testimony of the fact in our inmost consciousness which deceives not. They descend upon us, they dwell within us; for are we not being moved by their courage, earnestness, self-sacrifice, and love of country? Do we not feel supernaturally inspired and strengthened in our resolution to follow them and to complete the work they have so auspiciously started? Personally and individually, we may grieve over their being no more among us in their material garb, but super-personally our life is enriched and illuminated by their death.

We understand, therefore, by the immortality of the soul the perpetuation of spiritual life, not individually but supra-individually. The life runs in and through individuals, but it is more than the totality of them. It does not die with their annihilation, it survives them, and wears another garment of bodily existence, making itself ever younger, stronger, and nobler. In this sense, Japanese belief in the ancestral shades is justifiable. They are not really vanished in the haze of bygone ages; they are living in the freshness of youth in our midst, and what we worship is not their ghostly presence but their living spirit. Those who fell in the late war are not really fallen; they are still alive in the minds and hearts of their friends and worshipers. From the world of sense they are forever departed, but they have found their enduring home in the supra-individual realm. Their bones are crumbling in the dust, but their spirit is enkindled in our hearts. This, one of the plainest facts in the world, will be doubted only by those near-sighted, grossly material egoists who refuse to see the significance of human life.

I am by no means trying to cover the horrors and evils of war, for war is certainly hellish. Let us avoid it as much as possible. Let us settle all our international difficulties in a more civilized manner. But if it is unavoidable, let us go into it with heart and soul, with the firm conviction that our spiritual descendants will carry out and accomplish what we have failed personally to achieve. Let, therefore, the dead quietly repose in their last sleep. Nobody will dare stir their glorious ashes. As for us who are left behind, no superfluous words are in place, only we must not disgrace the honor and spirit of the dead who have solemnly bequeathed to us their work to perfect. Mere lamentation not only bears no fruit, it is a product of egoism, and has to be shunned by every enlightened mind and heart.

INDEX